Human
Wholeness

Human Wholeness

The Articles of Self Discovery

JOHN MEDDLING

authorHOUSE®

AuthorHouse™ LLC
1663 Liberty Drive
Bloomington, IN 47403
www.authorhouse.com
Phone: 1-800-839-8640

Published by AuthorHouse   07/22/2013

ISBN: 978-1-4817-7922-7 (sc)
ISBN: 978-1-4817-7923-4 (hc)
ISBN: 978-1-4817-7924-1 (e)

Library of Congress Control Number: 2013913111

Contents

About The Author

I have resided in Atlanta GA since 2002 where I am currently practicing as a license massage/neuromuscular therapist and serve as a health and wellness consultant. My work vary from photography, writing, electronic repair, serving as a life coach, motivational speaking and teaching. I have taught anatomy, physiology, pathology and many other medical subjects as a part of the massage program at Georgia Medical Institute for five years. My passion for health and wellness keeps me actively involved in a variety of medical and holistic research. I am a certified TESOL/TESL/TEFL (English teacher overseas) and am certified by Oxford Seminars based in Los Angeles California. I have taught Christian Education in one form or another for more than seventeen years. I am the father of one son, DeAndre.

Growing up in Nashville TN in a household with three brothers and three sisters and both parents—always led to spirited discussions. These discussions would range from boyfriends & girlfriends, sports, school, and the family favorite "the God questions" which fueled our recreational time as a family. I did not always get the answers I was looking for in those talks but these discussions sparked my curiosity to know and understand a mystical Intelligence. At the age of eleven I knew that I would be a seeker of truth—seeking for truth beyond the surface and not passively believing what someone else told me. It was seeing the diversities of beliefs in my family unit that made me curious about human behavior. If we (my siblings) were all raised by the same parents with the same value system, why was our behavior and belief so different from one another? Why was there a difference in our perception of God?

As a young adult I was always interested in human behavior and spent much of my time questioning the Universe. Questions about why people interact violently with one another over religious beliefs, and why was there so much confusion about who God is? Why is there so much controversy about who has the most accurate understanding of how God interact with man? How is it that most religions believe in one universal God but take issue with those who differ in worship and practice? These questions led me on a journey to understanding human behavior and God's interaction with man. Because I desired to understand the unique dichotomy between human beings, and humans relationship with God—I began surveying in a variety of social and religious groups. Through this observation I have found a non traditional path for my spirituality, and I am forever evolving into higher consciousness. My ideology is not considered as a mainstream belief system in most religious circles, but I am hoping it will challenge the readers to reevaluate and reaffirm their beliefs.

Thanks & Dedication

I believe that we are all mere reflections of the people we keep close company with, and if this is true then I am surrounded by some very special people. I owe my inspiration to all those who took the time to post their comments and encouragement to my website <jmselfdiscovery.com>. Thanks to my students at Georgia Medical Institute who took the time to complete the Lifestyle Surveys. Without their input, I would not have had the statistics to support many of my ideologies as it relates to relationships. Thanks to Linda George for reminding me to stay focus on my writing. Much appreciation for the McCoy family and the inspiration they brought to my writing. Linda McCoy, thank you for being my sounding board for topics and critiques. Had it not been for the supporters of my writings, I might have lost the enthusiasm to continue. Thank you for your positive influence and prayers. This book is dedicated to all of you.

Special thanks to: Dr. Reginald Turner for all your time and energy in critiquing and editing my work. Without your input and directions I would not have adequately expressed my thoughts in a comprehensible manner. Thank you so much for helping me to deliver this ideology to the world. May God richly bless you for the blessing you've been to me in your consistent support.

Also, special thanks to my brother Donald and **M DESIGNS** for the wonderful graphic art designs of this book's cover. Donald, you are truly gifted and I am so grateful and proud of the accomplishments you've made, and the many lives you have touched through your artwork and ministry.

Acknowledgements

I would like to express my appreciation to the many teachers of "consciousness" and creating with mind. Their teachings have contributed to my understanding of the active work of the human spirit and the power of thoughts. I want to express much appreciation to the online references that provided me with statistics and medical articles.

Thanks to:

Cristian C A Bodo article: The Biology of Sexual Orientation

H.O.M.E. Heterosexuals Organized for a Moral Environment.

Ann Harrington's article on the Placebo Affect

Wikipedia article entitled—Biology and Sexual Orientation

Jerry & Ester Hicks—Teachings of Abraham (The Law of Attraction) & The Vortex

Wayne Dyer—Power of Intentions

Marc David M.A.—Founder of Psychology of Eating Institute

Holly Pinafore—article: How your thoughts affect your metabolism

Mike Dooley—Thoughts Become Things (Choose Them Wisely) & Leveraging the Universe and Engaging the Magic

Rhonda Byrne—The Secrete

Napoleon Hill—Think and Grow Rich

Forward

This book will touch you at the very depth of your soul. Everyone needs someone to show them how to overcome their adversity—how to reframe and rethink their challenging situations in more positive, optimistic, and uplifting terms. Human Wholeness—The Articles of Self Discovery will teach you how to do all this and more.

Human Wholeness is soul talk. John Meddling's soul is talking directly and persuasively to your soul. His magnificent spirit reminds you that you have a magnificent spirit, too. He exalts you to rise up and overcome all that attempts to conquer you and instead to conquer it yourself. John teaches with tremendous wisdom how to be on top of your problems, situations, and circumstances rather than letting them be on top of you. Through this process, you learn to heal many of the broken and damaged parts of your life and restore to a place of wholeness.

John is a master storyteller. He writes in the gripping fashion of a best-selling novelist. He shares his own experiences of being caught in the quagmire of life's problems and tells how he swam to the edge of safety and success while never losing his humor, joy, and positive outlook on life. He does this with a radiant, robust smile and inspires you and teaches you to do the same.

John's lessons will make a positive, permanent difference in your life, your business, and your future. A book's value is not in how you feel when you read it, but more importantly, in how you can use it to handle your day-to-day situations, circumstances, and problems. John makes us believe that we can heal and grow. He fills us with the power of hope, happiness, encouragement, and the idea that "I am bigger than my biggest problem(s)."

This is a book that you will never forget. It will help you over and over again. I also predict that you will find the need to give it as a gift to those you love so that they too will be helped, inspired, and restored.

He is going to put a smile on your face, hope in your heart, and joy in your spirit!

Reginald H. Turner, Ph.D.

Introduction

Human Wholeness—The Articles of Self Discovery is John's ideology relating to the complexity of human behavior in relationships, and the individuals' absence of self worth that immobilizes spiritual growth. He expresses his opinions as to why people struggle with the ability to make clear and concise decisions, and why people struggle with their identity. He focuses on the reasons for human insecurities and how it affects the dynamics of living in higher consciousness. John expresses his thoughts on many biblical teachings that are frequently misunderstood or used out of context, as it relates to the subjects in his articles.

His sole purpose for this book is to enlighten its readers on the innate creative powers that dwell within each of us to assist in the acceleration of reaching our greatest potential. This book includes a compilation of expressions shared by individuals struggling with a variety of relationships issues and relationship dynamics, and who are challenged with their identity. These individuals vary in sexual orientation, religion, social status and politics. John has interviewed, consulted, and surveyed a range of people to establish facts about lifestyles, belief systems, and culture norms to name a few. He has had dialogue with many concerning their personal struggles with their identity. They range from religious leaders, political leaders, single parents, homosexuals, heterosexuals, and everyone in between. John believes that all people are seeking for "wholeness" whether they are conscious of it or not. He also believes that people are as whole, as they are aware and active in their responsibility to humanity. This responsibility to humanity consists of contributing to the growth and development of our society. The highest level of wholeness is reached when we commit to serving our fellowman with our talents, gifts and resources.

Regardless of what our titles, positions, age, sexual orientation, gender or spiritual beliefs, we all share the same basic need and host the same fears. We are all in pursuit of happiness, peace of mind, love and acceptance. We all seek wholeness on different levels, and we will only discover it when we tread the waters of self discovery.

For many years John has sought to understand his roles as a father, as a husband, and simply as a human being. He has asked, "How do I serve in each of these carnal or human roles and yet be a spiritual individual connected to Higher Intelligence?" The complexity of his humanity drove him to the exploration of self discovery. He believe that if he could only grasp an understanding of his own complexity, that he would better understand the people and world around him as well. So he went on the journey of studying and interviewing people of diverse sexual orientations, ages, gender, religious beliefs, races, and cultures. His curiosity of human behavior led him into associations that heightened his social awareness. As John engaged into these diverse environments where there were differences in beliefs, he began to discover his "true self" in the person of a spiritual being. He became validated in his own belief systems, and began to understand that the contrast of other people lives helped him shape his own life. So the information that you will find in this book is a compilation of others experiences as well as John's ideology. He serves as a messenger in some of the topics—but most of the expressions reflect his own ideology. Because he is ever evolving, relearning and breaking away from old belief systems—he reserves the right to change his opinions and views in upcoming materials.

When we understand our individuality and live accordingly, we will eliminate some of the frustrations that we encountered in our relationship with ourselves and with others. Having a healthy perception of ones self is the foundation for true appreciation for the social world that surrounds us. Often we find fault in the other person when our relationships fail. Perhaps when we fail to comprehend the complexity of our human nature and individual need to fulfill ourselves—we are lead into misconceptions of other's actions, words and deeds in the relationship. Failure to understand the dynamics of one's self often bring relationships to their demise.

As individuals seeking to understand one's self or individuality, we must first examine ourselves and discover what really makes us tick. We must conclude the reason(s) for our passivity or aggressiveness, dependency upon others or independence. Why do we require so much attention or why is it that we fail to appreciate attention when it is shown to us? What makes some people competitive and others complacent? These are just a few questions that we might be challenged by—but it can relate to any other behavior that prevents us from being in harmony with ourselves and the world around us. It is in the observation of one's self that these questions should be answered—revealing the essence of our *being* that will leads us into the bliss of understanding personal wholeness. Wholeness is experienced when we understand the dynamics of ourselves first—and then sharing that knowledge to the world.

Our purpose as human beings should not be to merely exist—being led by negative perceptions and carried away by our fears and insecurities. Humanity is beckoned to a higher level of consciousness and a greater sense of self awareness that will ultimately deliver us into wholeness. In these article throughout this book, John is expressing that we are indeed made in the image and nature of God, the Highest Intelligence, and essence of all life. It is in the hope of this belief that the contents of this book will enlighten and allow you to see yourselves in a more majestic, empowering, and self loving way. Our relationships will become more productive when we obtain wholeness within ourselves. When we experience personal wholeness, we will become healed in our spirit, healed in our soul, and healed in our bodies.

Article 1

Who Am I

The question that should be asked to begin the process of self discovery that will ultimately lead to understanding personal wholeness is "Who Am I?" Who we are in core perspective will vary from person to person, depending on our frame of references and life experiences. Everything we've experienced has made us who we are today. It becomes a matter of being able to properly decipher these experiences in order to fairly discern and access the world around us.

Let us identify with the complexity of our humanity. As human beings we consist of body, mind, and spirit. Our bodies reflect our physical aspect, and the mind reflects intellect, and our spirit is the eternal, all knowing guiding force within us. The spirit is often defined as intuition, perceptivity or instinct and it is simply the God part of our humanity that leads humans into perfect decision making.

Our body simply serves as the shell that houses the mind (intellect) but our spirit (the God aspect indwelling us) on the other hand serves as our internal guiding force navigating us into higher consciousness. It is as the spirit beckoning from the subconscious—and awakening the conscious mind. It introduces the supernatural revelation to human intellect. If we take away the mind and body (as in death), the spirit would remain—for it is our essence. I will go a step further and say that the spirit is the God aspect indwelling our physical bodies, and is heard through the voice of our subconscious. I believe that we as humans are innately more spiritual beings than we are physical beings. I believe that we existed in spirit long before we took on physical bodies. The Bible states: *"Before I shaped you in the womb, I knew all about you. Before you saw the light of day, I had holy plans for you . . ."* (Jeremiah 1:5 The Message Bible). I also believe that innately we are more God based than we are human, but the socialization from living as human beings has disconnected us from the essence of who we are. Our spirit or "God aspect" has no need for food, shelter, or clothing because it is eternal and it is our essence and it is Source. Spirit never dies just as God never ceases to exist.

Our physical bodies however require physical substance in order to be sustained—substances such as food, shelter, and clothing. Humans are so intricately designed that we must be conscious of how we take care of the physical body. Therefore, making good health decisions as it relates to what we eat and drink and healthy activities, will directly affect a physiological change in our bodies. We know that toxic foods and behaviors such as illegal drug use can impair good judgment. Ignoring healthy lifestyles alone can cloud good decision making, and will negatively affect the communication between our conscience mind and spirit. Therefore, understanding the relationship between our physiology, psyche and spirit—we should take extra care in the maintenance of our physical bodies. It is vital to the balance of our human complexity that we live in harmony with our whole *being* by observing the well-being of the body, mind and spirit. It is not enough to simply eat healthy to preserve the body, but in addition taking time to relax and restoring the mind is a crucial element in being whole. When the mind is relaxed, the voice of the Spirit which is the all knowing guiding force—can be heard in our consciousness.

Our mind is comprised of intellect, emotions, intentions, purpose, objectivity, desire, and opinions. It is the home of where our lifetime experiences and frame of reference live. Too often the decisions of our lives are made from here—sometimes to our detriment when seeking spiritual answers to non-logical matters (such as matters of the heart), which is solely the job of the Spirit. The mind is the vehicle through which our logical decisions are made. If we are to fully enjoy this earthly experience, we must reconnect to our Source/ God which is spiritual.

When we bring these three components of our humanity together, and analyze their relationship to one another and gain an understanding of their dynamics, it can enlighten us to the specific areas in which we are infirmed. Understanding these three components of our *being* will unlock the doors to who we are.

There is another aspect of "Who Am I." This hinges upon the understanding that we as human beings are a compilation of thoughts about self confined in any given moment. To further elaborate, when we perceive ourselves to be in a situation—we trap that perception into that present moment making it a reality. For example, when a person win a million dollar lottery—they instantly see themselves as a millionaire. But nothing has physically changed around them in that moment. That person however is now experiencing psychological (mind) change in their perception of *self*. Their mindset went from lack to abundance, and their image of *self* became illuminated by the new reality of being a millionaire. Who we are is determined by the thoughts we hold at any given moment—and not by circumstances. We do not need a million dollars to live in the mindset of a millionaire. If we seek wealth, good health, a better job or any other thing—we must see ourselves already possessing it. Daydream about having what you want, putting yourself in the mindset of already owning it—and it will find its way to you. It is in the present that we are or become what we believe ourselves to be. *As a man thinks in his heart, so is he* (Proverbs 23:7 KJV).

It is crucial to our spiritual growth that a paradigm shift about ourselves is made in each moment of our life. We must envision ourselves as possessing whatever we desire with the concept of having it NOW! No one can determine who we are but us. The life we desire is held ransom by the beliefs we hold about ourselves. Nothing can affect us unless we give permission to it. So live in the awareness of possessing all good things NOW! The awareness of who I am in this present moment can define "Who Am I."

Article 2

Understanding the Conscious and Subconscious *Self*

The enlightening of the conscious and subconscious *self* is the foundation of understanding where Higher Intelligence becomes intertwined with humanity. People have asked me, "How do I know when God is speaking to me?" My answer is always prefaced with the belief that human beings are multifaceted in personalities but all share the same spiritual Source—meaning that we all possess one "all knowing spirit" that we call God or Higher Intelligence, wired into our *being*. It is in the awareness of the subconscious self or spirit that God or Higher Intelligence abides. We know when God speaks to us when we are able to hear the voice of concise information coming from within us—from our subconscious *self*. Sometime this information may not make sense to our analytical minds but we *feel* a certainty of truth about it.

There are four aspects of the conscious *self* and they are rationalization, convictions, perception and ego. The conscious self is the part of us that has learned behaviors as to what is appropriate and inappropriate—it consists of the values taught to us as children by parents, teachers or anyone who influenced our life. The conscious self might be better understood as the mind—the rationalizing aspect of our being. We are naturally rational and analytical *beings*, and can readily tap into our value system which is formed in childhood. Our value system then creates the convictions that we hold as to what is appropriate or inappropriate. For example: If our parents taught us as children not to steal, it would be ingrained that stealing is wrong. Our consciousness *self* would have adopted the belief that stealing was inappropriate behavior. The conscious self is analytical and perceives the world through the eyes of logic and makes decisions based on what it has been taught to believe as appropriateness. The conscious reasoning is the natural or superficial human way of thinking. Sometimes it becomes foggy in its ability to discern right from wrong—often being governed by ones' perception. Perceptions are also formed by what we are taught to believe as appropriate, and everyone has their own opinions about what is appropriate. So everyone's perception will be different from another because no two people perceive or understand things exactly the same. The human ego is also found in the conscious self. This is where debates and disagreements with others, who views are in opposition to ours, are formulated. In our ego there is little tolerance for differences, and offences become apparent when what we have been taught as acceptable is challenged. The conscious self because of the ego factor can be prideful and threatened when beliefs are questioned. Feelings and emotions are weaved into this aspect of self, which subjects human beings to erroneous beliefs and misconstrued perceptions.

Now on the other hand, the subconscious self or spirit (where I believe God abides) is the heightened consciousness that humans are yet learning to tap into. Often we have heard the term in the religious world as "walking in the spirit" in reference to heightened consciousness. The subconscious self is the spiritual aspect of human beings. It is God hidden in our human characteristics—and this essence embodies all truth. Whereas the conscious self has four aspects, the subconscious self has only one—and that is "truth" or "knowing." It serves as the home where God abides within humans and where God gives supernatural guidance and insight into every aspect of our lives. The subconscious self is not analytical but simply "knowing," and it is absolute. The subconscious self or spirit as we stated earlier, is perfectly clear in every regard and in every situation—never requiring counseling or guidance for it is indeed the Higher Intelligence, the God of the universe, making abode within our human vessels. Hearing and understanding the voice of the subconscious self or voice of God has to be learned through experiences and practice—unlike the conscious self or mind that comes more naturally because it is connected to our learned behaviors. This is why I believe people fail to hear the voice of Higher Intelligence clearly—because there is often a need to analyze from human prospection what is spiritually being introduced. The wisdom of Higher Intelligence cannot be analyzed by the mere conscious self—for the conscious self is void of spiritual clarity in its nature. "*The natural man cannot understand the things of God for they will appear to him as foolishness—neither can he know them because they are spiritually discerned.*" (1 Corinthians 2:14 paraphrased)

We must awaken our conscious senses to the reality of our subconscious self (the spirit) in order to hear the voice, the directions, and the wisdom of God. When we become more accustom to living from the wisdom of our subconscious self—our God aspect, we will experience the peace that innately becomes us—the peace we experienced as infants. We will not find ourselves worrying over matters in this life, but will live in the calmness that everything is always well with us. When we live in the reality of our subconscious self we become more at ease with the behaviors of those who oppose us. We will never have to seek out success for it will always find us. Living through this awareness of self is where human beings were perfectly meant to live. This is how God infiltrates the consciousness of the world through a paradigm shift. If all of humanity could only connect to the Source abiding within it, how blissful and wonderful life would be.

Article 3

Power of the Subconscious

Some people are more focused on the material aspects of their lives rather than the spiritual or subconscious aspects. We often negate the power of the spiritual forces that govern our lives that manifests from the subconscious to our conscious and into our realty. The conscious mind focuses on the tangible or material world of reality while the subconscious communicates with the spiritual or unseen world. Our subconscious brings the unseen into the realm of the seen/reality. Higher Intelligence communicates divinely through the subconscious mind—for it is Gods spirit or our essence working through us creating our realities. We can actually say that our subconscious is the God of the Universe intertwined into our humanity making up our essence. Therefore, we should take notice of the things we draw into our lives by our conscious actions and suggestions. We innately possess the power to summon from our subconscious which enables us to operate as creators in manifesting what we want. Because of our innate divinity, what we think about or focus upon comes into our reality. However, we must see ourselves as divine entities operating through the human experience—understanding that we are expressions of God manifested in human form. This is why we as human beings have such a strong desire to thrive and excel, to live with purpose, to love, and to create after our kind. When we see ourselves from the divine perspective, we will empower our lives, by the work of the subconscious mind, and will create the life that innately reflects our divinity.

This is why I also believe that visualization is so important in manifesting the things we want. When the subconscious is triggered, we bring into our conscious focus the lifestyles, the love relationships, the job or career and the spiritual experiences that we wish to have. The purpose of the conscious mind is to make observations, create desires, seek out strategies and move in the direction of the things wanted. However, the subconscious is working outside of our intellect to bring into existence our desires and wishes. When we understand the concept that the unseen forces within us are in operation aiding us in our creation, we can take pride in our deliberate manifestation of good things. There must be an alignment of the conscious and subconscious mind in order for creation to be speedy. This alignment takes place when our "natural mind" the conscious, comes into agreement with the "spiritual mind" the subconscious. Some religious people might term this as "Walking in the spirit."

When we become clearly focused, directing our attention and energy on the things we want—allowing visualization to spark that sense of anticipation, until we feel as if we're already possessing the things that we desire—we will then speed up the creating process. Life is meant to be enjoyed, and we are meant to possess all that we desire, but failing to understanding how to manifest the abundance in our lives will leave us unfulfilled and disappointed. We suspend our joy when our conscious mind is void of the understanding of God indwelling us. A sense of powerlessness and hopelessness taints our *sense of self* when there is no recognition of God in the conscious aspect of our *being*. It should be noted that the manifestations in people lives are slow or sometimes nonexistent when they fail to understand the power of walking in the awareness of their divinity. We shouldn't have to continue living with this sense of lack and being unfulfilled. We need only to live in the reality of God consciousness which brings all good things into our reality. After all, God lives, moves and think through us—and we are empowered when we recognize it.

Article 4

Reconnecting to Source

It is imperative that an understanding is established about who or what "Source" is. When talking about reconnecting to "Source," I am speaking of connecting to God, Higher Intelligence, Creator of The Universe, or whatever name you choose that define who God is to you. I do not relate to God by gender because I personally do not believe that God as Higher Intelligence can be confined to gender or anything else that's physical.

In order to understand our connection to Source, we must maintain a comprehension of facts that first of all there is absolutely no way for human beings to be disconnected from Source. "Source" is the essence of who we all are, wrapped in human form only in experiential levels and dimensions. To put this in layman terms, all human beings possess a quality of God, or attributes that reflects the divine nature of God—that I believe makes up the essence of our *being*. Some people acquire more of the "perceived" characteristics of God because they have learned to master their lives through proper teaching and supernatural insight. As a result of a person mastering their life, they live more harmoniously, possess deeper insight, seem unbothered by life's disappointments and overall have a good emotional balance. Our experiences in life teach us who or what Source is, along with the revelation of who we are as spiritual *beings*. When we understand our relationship to "Source," we can then know that human beings and Source/ God are inseparable.

Since humans beings are inseparable from Source, the question arises "Why don't I get what I need from Source if we are inseparable, and why am I always lacking?" I believe that we fail to obtain the things we need or want because the communication network between us and Source is blocked. Since we are inseparable and are one with Source, could it simply be that we are out of tune with ourselves? Could it be that failing to understand our *God ability*, that we forfeit the things that are rightly ours? Human Beings have the creative ability to draw the supernatural into the natural. Often our sense of feeling unworthy hinders the process. Many of us have been taught to believe that this sense of unworthiness is humility, but it is not. If anything, unworthiness is more connected to the lack of faith—feelings of not deserving.

If the essence of who we are is God—then how can we believe that God in us, clothed in human form is undeserving? We must realize that when we request (by way of prayer) anything of God, we are only giving permission to ourselves to have those things we are petitioning. We do not have to ask for permission to get what we want, but simply *summons* and *allow* those things to come into our lives. As co-creators with God who lives within us—we are able to manifest the supernatural into the natural. It is God working through our humanity that brings to us all that we seek. We are not being arrogant when making these claims but walking in the awareness of "The Source" within us. Until we grasp the essence of our greatness as human beings, there will always be a lack of manifestations in our lives.

The thought of mankind being one with God may sound like blasphemy in the ears of religious people, but this ideology is referred to many times in the Bible. Jesus himself expressed this same belief in St. John 10: 30-31 by saying that "I and my Father/God are one." Jesus' statement was perceived as arrogance by the Jews, so they took up stones to kill him. This is no reflection on the Jews because many people today share the same sentiment that we are not God and that God is not us. Higher Intelligence is ingeniously hidden within our human dynamics—to the point that we are inseparable from our divinity. Until we identify with the divinity within us, we will never experience the unlimited bliss and manifestation of our true self.

Reconnecting to our Source is simply a matter of a paradigm shift of one's image of *self* and the understanding of the dynamics of the God & human relationship.

> *How a man sees his life is based on the treasure he finds in himself—when he finds the God within—he finds the wholeness of his life.*
>
> J. Meddling

Article 5

The Power of Emotions

Our emotions are probably the most misunderstood aspect of our humanity. Even within ourselves there's confusion about why we feel and act the way we do. People tend to feel bad or guilty when unwanted situations surface, and yet we feel excitement and joy when all is going well. Our emotions are the guiding sensory that connects us to God, and God communicates or guide us through our sensory of feelings. This leads into supernatural insight of our purpose for *self* and to humanity—which is connected to our own will. Our emotions are wired into our humanity and yet serve as a spiritual force of guidance. This force of guidance cannot be mistaken or misunderstood by our subconscious *self*, because it is the God aspect of our being. It is God expressing through us in the form of our emotions. The only reason that emotions are misunderstood is because many are out of touch with their *inner self* or divinity.

There are actually only two categories of emotions—the one that makes you feel good and the other that makes you feel bad. There is absolutely nothing in between. We are inclined to give our emotions all kinds of names such as anger, frustration, loneliness, sadness hopelessness and fear. These are all emotions that we consider as bad. On the other hand, we have what we consider as our good emotions which are: happiness, cheerfulness, peace, excitement, and love. It doesn't matter the name we give our emotions, but it is important to know that all emotions give insight as to where we are in harmony with ourselves. Our emotions give insight to what we are continuously thinking about or where our "thought energy" is being focused. To further simplify the term "thought energy" is to say that our emotions follow our thoughts—producing our realities.

An example of how "thought energy" works—might be better understood by this example: We have all experienced a persons' mood or vibes without verbal communication—where their energy projected to us that they were not friendly or either didn't care to be bothered. We are able to discern people moods and vibes because of the output of their energy—we make this observation without hardly any effort. The energy that we experience with others is simply *the God* within us trying to connect with the God in them. Unfortunately, people are not always on the same energy output level of God awareness as one another. As a result of not being on the same *output* level of awareness, we find ourselves out of harmony with one another.

In Christian circles we relate to a person who is able to discern the energy, spirit or vibe of other's as possessing the gift of discernment—but in actuality we all possess this ability. Some people are more in tuned or discerning of these energies than others. If we were to become more in tune with our *inner selves*, we would also become more discerning of others. In order to understand the behavior of others, we should first understand *self*. It is the awakening of Higher Intelligence manifesting in our human form, via our emotions—that makes the world around us more easily understood. Not only does the emotion projects energy, but also have the ability to attract like or similar energy to it. An example of this is when we think continuously about something we may, or may not want in our lives, and it shows up in our reality. This is the science or work of energy attracting to itself, like a magnet attracting another magnet that's in magnetic force with it. Through our emotions, we as humans are doing the same thing whether we are conscience of it or not. If we do not want bad experiences as a part of our realities, then we should not allow ourselves to wallow in our bad emotions. But if we are seeking more joy and positivity in our lives, then we should focus on our good emotions.

The power of our emotion has the ability to drastically influence our lives in whatever direction we choose to travel. We must make our choices wisely by allowing the *inner self* to connect with the God of the Universe—who guides us through all of life experiences by way of our emotions.

> **Our life today is the manifestations of the things we sought in our past.**
>
> J. Meddling

Article 6

Courage to Face Yourself

Foolish is the man who looks into a mirror and refuses to recognize the image he sees.

J. Meddling

When we as human beings allow ourselves to love and except our individuality and not be so judgmental of ourselves, we began to live in the power of our *inner self*. It indeed takes courage to face who we really are. Confronting the insecurities that lies within all of us can challenge the self validation of who we are as individuals. Self-esteem can be compromised when consumed with the convictions of how we should be—judging ourselves based upon other's expectations of us. Therefore, it makes no difference how affluent or influential we appear to others—because internally we are our greatest critics. Because we are aware of our own failures, indiscriminate activities, our prejudices, and the people that we may have secretly wronged—we become heavily weighed with our convictions. This can and usually causes fear or the uneasiness of facing one's self. Often, we are not even aware that we fear or feel uncomfortable about who we are, until someone who knows us personally tells us about ourselves in a moment of rage. Unconsciously we feel that if we ignore the *superficial self*, (the part of our humanity that thrives to appease the opinions of others) that we can justify our *wholeness* by telling ourselves that we are OK. The reality is we become whole and complete, strong and mature, graceful and humble in character, when we come clean to who we really are, and face our insecurities.

One of the dangers of not recognizing ourselves for who we really are makes us vulnerable to the pitfall of believing that we are invincible. If we believe that we are invincible we become susceptible to delusion. We may never see the detriment that we are bringing upon ourselves until it is too late to make a change. If we refuse to face our insecurities, the result of this delusion may affect all who are subordinate or in relationship to us—children, spouse, and employees to name a few. We often see this with a leader of a country who is engulfed with his or her own pride—enforcing rules and regulations that do not benefit the people—only feeding the ego of that leader's reputation and power. Unfortunately, the consequences of the decisions made by a proud and arrogant leader is trickled down to the innocent who are subordinate—now becoming victims of their leaders' marks of insecurity. Too many nations suffer as a result of having pious leaders. These are leader's who would rather appear right—when they know that they are wrong, simply to keep from acknowledging their own inabilities at the cost and detriment of innocent people. The same is true in families where a parent refuses to admit a wrong to a child—and the child grows up believing that the wrong, is right.

To refuse to face *self* is to deny Higher Intelligence the opportunity to manifest and express wholeness through our human form. God touches the lives of a nation through its leaders, but if the leaders are led astray by their own insecurities or indulgences so will the nation follow. However, I believe that there will always be a remnant of people in wayward nations who will find the joy of life regardless of flawed leadership. This remnant will seek for truth and guidance within themselves and they shall find it. The same is true in the family unit.

Even as parents we should take courage in facing our fears and insecurities. Sometime our children should hear us say that "Even though I am the parent, I do not proclaim to be perfect." Our children should know that we have fears and insecurities, but be taught how to triumphantly face them. Let's not hinder the emotional and creative growth of our children by being too proud to be wrong sometimes.

Parents must sometimes become vulnerable with their children by teaching the lessons that no one is above correction and that inner growth should always be priority. When children are taught the value of facing the realities within themselves, they will develop a healthy social perspective about the world around them and the world within themselves. This understanding is applicable to all relationships and not just leaders or parents.

We will always evolve to a higher consciousness when we release our inner and social fears. Therefore, on a daily basis we should be ready to take courage in facing ourselves, conquering our inner fears about *self*, and challenging old belief systems that derived from ancient societies which may not be relevant for our time. We are the image in the mirror—do not be afraid to face it!

The greatest fears to face are the fears associated with ones' self. If we will harness the loving memories of the image in the mirror, we will negate the terror of our hearts.

J. Meddling

Article 7

The Power of "Self"

I believe that the universal world is constantly changing and adapting to the requests and needs of human beings. The irony is that we neither recognize nor understand the impression we're having on the world around us. Every day the world is expanding its arms of provision upon every new life that comes into it. The Universe, being understood as God or Higher Intelligence is in constant acquaintance with the human spirit. The Universe is revealing more of itself through our human instrumentalities. When we understand that we are the physical expression of God in the earth, we'll be able to take our places as the conscious co-creators of the universe. The perceived mysteries of God is unfolding before our very eyes revealing who we are through the person of God, as well as revealing who God is through the person we are. We need to know that humans and God are one. The Holy Bible confirms this in St. John 17:21 which reads: "that they may all be one; even as you, Father are in Me and I in you, that they may also be in Us . . ."(New American Standard). In other words, as God and Jesus are one—having the same focal point in harmony—let all human beings also possess the same mindset of harmony and "oneness." Being "one" is identified in that scripture as having the same focus or intentions. As I stated earlier—we are all co-creators with God, and all of us have the ability to bring into our reality whatever we desire. It is the God of the Universe within us, providing us the means to do our daily actions and to bring into our reality whatever desired.

Understanding and utilizing the power that lies within *self* will propel us to a supernatural level of living in authority. We will be able to thrive with certainty as we pursue our destiny in life. We can live as deliberate and conscious creators, knowing that the experiences in our lives have been summoned and not just encountered. Humans were not created to merely exist upon the earth without having control of anything—living life by chance, or surviving on a limb and prayer. We were created to thrive and conquer our dreams and ambitions—to live life in abundance with joy and bliss. Unfortunately many will not gravitate to this higher God given call, because many will never get beyond the survival mentality. The *inner self* must be elevated to God consciousness or God mindedness—the ability to think creatively as God. When we esteem our *inner self*, we in turn exalt the God who resides within us. The Holy Bible states in reference to this fact: "You are from God little children and have overcome them; because greater is God who is in you than he who is in the world." (1 John 4:4 New American Standard.) We are not diluting the authenticity or power of God by esteeming ourselves, but rather, giving credence to our connection to divinity.

When we fail to understand the power of *self*, we tend to except whatever comes into our reality. Some might even feel that it is being humble, excepting things into their lives that they do not want—but this way of thinking is degrading to the intelligence of God, who enables us to create the reality that we desire for ourselves. It is God that commanded the first *perceived* humans, Adam and Eve to take dominion over every living thing that moved on the earth (Genesis 1: 28), which included taking charge over *self*. Our duty is to take the gift of life and multiply it in the unique way that we see fit as individuals. Jesus tells the parable of the talents, in Mathew 25: 14-30; and just like the characters in that story, many of us are wasting the "talent" of our life by not managing/creating our own lives. There are so many people who feel that someone else would do a better job managing/ creating their lives for them. This is why people seek out other to give them directions in things in which only they (the one seeking directions) have the answer. Sometimes it might be a pastor, a parent or even a best friend that you would seek the opinion of in knowing what direction you should take for your life. On life decisions, no one is better equipped with that information than you. Consequently, when we place the authority of our lives into the hands of others—often we are directed onto a path that is not in harmony with our true desires. When people feel that they will mess up their own lives and therefore render it to another, they loose their divine creativity.

We come into this existence as a willing *being* ready to navigate our journey through life. But some of us become homogenized from our true divine nature with the fears projected upon us by others who are unsure of their own creative ability. Many have forgotten that their responsibility in this existence is to experiment and enjoy all of the splendors and experiences that come with learning who they are as co-creators. I do not believe that the Creative God of the Universe is holding us hostage to a man-made belief system, critiquing our every move and action. Nor do I believe God to be an angry man keeping an account of the bad and good that humans do. However, I do believe that every human soul is given the power to orchestrate their own destiny through self perception. We are created and infiltrated with the wisdom that comes from the highest of all intelligence—that intelligence being God. So let's take joy in basking in the fullness of all that our lives have to offer us—and let us enjoy the developing gifts that resides within all of us, and through all humanity.

> *If we are to imitate the greatness of Higher Intelligence, we must first identify with the power residing within ourselves—and live in the reality of that power.*
>
> J. Meddling

Improving Your Life by Organizing Your Surroundings

In a class discussion about self improvement a student asked me, "Mr. Meddling, what has been the most important factor for improving your life?" Without reservation I answered, "Organizing my surroundings." Most people will never see the relevance of an organized environment as it relates to an improved life, but as we organize our personal living space, we also systematize things in our psyche. In my observation, people who live in messy surroundings usually have problems with managing their finances, managing their time, making clear and precise decisions, and discipline with eating. This lack of organization can be a mirror into the mindset of the people who fail to complete or even start things in their life. Disorganization is definitely a mindset or mentality that hinders the creativities of the human soul. When we are cluttered mentally or emotionally, we tend to loose that inner drive for progression. When our personal surroundings are unorganized, and when we are constantly faced with unfinished projects that we once started, they often weigh as *incompletes* in our psyche. These *incompletes* can hinder our ability to be creative and to move forward. Incomplete tasks are marked in our subconscious as a failure, leaving us with a sense of not being able to achieve. This is the reason why many lack the confidence to start anything new because the *old* or incomplete lie before them unaccomplished.

Individuals who lack organizational skills typically have problems with maintaining a healthy diet—for it takes a certain level of discipline to eat properly. Poor dieting leads to poor energy levels, which lead to poor exercising habits, which leads to poor health, which leads to a potentially shorter life. Of course I'm not saying that ALL unorganized people are in poor health, but I do believe that our surroundings affect our ability to be mentally clear. I feel that the discipline we as individuals wish to achieve in our lives should first be reflected in our personal surrounding. I believe that our ability to be successful in life is directly connected to the harmony of our environment.

Not only is diet affected, but relationships are also affected by cluttered minded individuals. This is not to be taken as an insult, but simply mean that the person whose surroundings is unharmonious, are often out of balance with their *inner self*, which is always in rapport with God who gives us our wholeness. When people are out of harmony with *self*, they're usually out of harmony with the world and people around them. Once again, this is not to say that ALL unorganized people are out of touch with the world around them or that they all have unharmonious relationships, but to simply point out that disorganization lends to many other areas of disconnect and non accomplishments.

Harmonizing our environment to our creative *spirit* brings perfect synergy to the body/mind connection and will ultimately connect us to our divinity. We are always affected on a spiritual level by our surroundings because the things around us feed into our human energies. We should strive to maintain that inner peace by organizing our surroundings. Organization perpetuates the inner peace that opens our awareness to the creative Intelligence of the Universe. The creative Intelligence within us is organizing the material world around us. This creative Intelligence is God manifested in the *inner you*. Therefore, the world/environment around you is your creative work.

When Manifestation Is Slow

It can be exhausting and even frustrating having to wait on something that you feel you must have right now. Especially when so much energy has been exerted and we've poured our hearts into believing and expecting for something or someone to come into our life, and manifestation is still slow. Often we believe so deeply for the *thing* or person that we become discouraged when what we want does not manifest. Questions of our worthiness or the pureness of our faith is challenged, so we loose heart thinking that we've done something wrong to cause the Universe not to respond to our request. We often hear people say in such cases that "If it's God's will or "in God's time" things will happen for us. This is what I believe to be a sad resignation of putting off and getting the things we need or want. None of these statements of reservation are true—for we do not exist in this world to prove our worthiness or to reach a higher level of righteousness. We are "righteous" in this very moment because we are born innately righteous. In our present state, we are the expression of God in human form, but we exist in this earthly realm to live out the human experience as God on earth. I believe our true purpose is to live our natural lives with the supernatural assistance of the Universe already abiding within us. We are to simply live our individual lives in harmony with God who resides harmoniously within our human frames.

So when manifestation is slow, there are usually only a few factors involved. The first is what I relate to as conflicting beliefs. A conflicting belief is when your personal belief system is in conflict with what you want. For example, if you desire to be a millionaire but you believe rich people only become rich by cheating and stealing, but you do not believe in cheating or stealing to have success—that would be a conflicting belief. Your framework of thinking would have to change to "Rich people work hard and honest to achieve their success and I am willing to work hard and honest to gain my success." Now you are in congruency or agreement with your personal belief system and you are ready to manifest the things you desire. But when your desires conflict with what you believe as to how you are to obtain what is wanted, your belief system is in conflict. The beliefs that dominate your emotions is the one that will govern your manifestation, because your belief system dictates the emotions associated with that thought which will consequently affect the manifestation. We will not manifest productively if our belief system is in opposition of our inner convictions. Our beliefs, and the emotion associated with that belief must be congruent to one another. When these premises of belief and emotions are in conflict, we often get a mixture of what we want and what we **do not want**—but never manifesting exactly what's desired.

The second factor is not focusing clearly on the desired manifestation. Too often we are distracted by our current circumstances that dictate our emotional *frequency* which affects the creation process. Our focus or imagination helps us to bring into clear view what it is that we truly want. This is where I believe vision boards and day-dreaming plays a role in the creation process. Having a visual of what's desired heightens the belief and expectancy of the thing wanted. Having this visual also gives us a sense of ownership even when we do not yet possess the object of desire. This is a very basic understanding in automotive sales. The salesman allows you to drive the car, work the controls, and in some cases allow you to keep the car overnight to get a sense of ownership of it. The salesman usually asks the potential buyer "Can you see yourself in this car?" Once we commit to liking that car and seeing ourselves in it, the salesman hones on the close of the sale. The Universe does the exact same thing. When the Universe sees that we have a strong focused interest in something, the Universe/ God goes to work to bring it into fruition.

The third component of slow manifestation but not necessarily the last factor is the lack of desire. There are many reasons that people lack the desire of having anything better. Some may feel a sense of unworthiness, while others are unwilling to exert the energy needed to obtain their prize because it cause for too much work. Others might feel that life is not meant to be abundant, so in that lack of understanding, they settle for whatever comes into their life. Yet, many others may simply lack patience and become discouraged and their desire began to wane. Lacking desire will destroy the need to day-dream or to have imaginations of a life that is grand. Lack of desire can and will destroy one's need to have a vision for their life. This is why so many people simply exist in life but never truly live life. Their life is aimless meaning that they have no goal to reach or vision to fulfill—and "Where there is no vision, the people perish:" (Proverbs 29:18). Where there is no vision, people will cast off the restraints of the law—and the law I speak of is the universal law that all mankind is made in the image or *spirit* of God. We are ALL innately divine—possessing the ability to be great and to do great things. But if there's no desire, there will be no creative energy that will ultimately lead to the life of true fulfillment. Absence of desire—is where we perish in our complacency. However, we are able to heighten our desire by simply focusing or even pretending by means of day dreaming about what we want. Heighten desire can help us regain the clear focus needed to manifest the things we are seeking. Heighten desire provides the magnetic attracting power that bring the unseen realities into the tangible realm.

Desire is the component that sets the pace of human lives. This is to say that (in most cases that I've observed) those who have much are those who have desired much. On the other hand, those who experienced lack and deprivation in their lives, lack the tenacity to strive and work hard for what they want. Some even lacked the desire to possess more than what they have because they feel that they would not remain humble if they had excess. There is a direct collation between desiring to work hard for what you want and obtaining. This does not mean that all work is physical in its pursuit in obtaining, but can also be a spiritual work stemming from the supernatural realm. For example: The exercise of thinking outside of the box, thinking in God consciousness or in the awareness that you, like God—have the ability to create your own world. Being aware and understanding that God is residing in you, is a spiritual work by itself. The Universe will never let you down if only you send the clear message of your heart's desire. Never give up on your goals or dreams because the Universe is always creating through you, the world around you—just as you perceive it to be.

Article 10

Overcoming Abuses

Often when we think of overcoming abuse, we think of someone who is the victim of some sort of drug addiction, violence, or someone who has mistreatment imposed upon them. Of course these are all abuses but I have found that some of the worse cases of abuses are self imposed. The abuse that I'm speaking of in this article relates to self imposed abuse that comes as a result of not understanding who you are. I believe that people are often more critical and more torturous upon themselves than anyone else could ever be. When we as human beings fail to see ourselves as powerful creative beings with the assistance of Higher Intelligence or God—is when self esteem issues creep in giving place to self abuse. Because, failing to recognize the authority we possess as spiritual creative beings causes us to subject ourselves to bad habits and addictions that are not of our conscious creation. None of us would purposely place ourselves in an uncomfortable situation if we were aware of what we were doing. But what's unfortunate is that many of us do not understand how it is that we attract these abusive situations into our lives. People who are, and remain in abusive situations are often victims of themselves long before they become abused by someone else.

Abusive behavior of one's self stems from the mindset of the person who is unaware of their true essence—experiencing insecurities with the *inner self*. One of the most profound reasons that people live in insecurity is that they fail to recognize their purpose in life. When we fail to understand our true purpose, self abuse is almost inevitable. Those who abuse others are also unaware of the divine authority and power that they possess within themselves. Abusers feel the need to physically impose their power upon another in identifying their own authority. The one who abuses others is just like the one whom abuses themselves in that neither understands that they are victims unto themselves, being governed by their own fears and insecurities. And their healthy perception of *self* is lost in that same fear and insecurity. Therefore, the act of controlling another is a manifestation of fear. The abuser (whether self imposed or imposing upon another), does not realize his/her lack of connection with the elevated and spiritual aspect of their own *being*. But if there was recognition of one's true essence—the aspect of our divinity, there would be no need or desire to control another. Recognition of one's divinity is what I believe to be the greatest paradigm shift in humanity.

The abused person, on the other hand is also the recipient of their own inner fears. This is especially true if they remain in the abusive situation. When the abused person is elevated to a higher consciousness of *self*, they will love themselves enough to change their situation. Even in critical situations where someone else is depending on the abused individual for protection—in the case of a child whose safety might be the issue—the abused person will make strategic changes for the protection of their child. They will not live in the deception that things will automatically get better. When the abused become aware of their true essence which is the God aspect of our *being*—he or she will always make the right decision.

Problems do not automatically improve or become corrected in abusive situations when no proactive decision is made. Usually the fear element of what the abuser might do if they (the abused person) become proactive, is often the crippling factor that fuses them into the situation. The abuser and the abused are both victims living out the manifestation of their own inner fears. One is thinking about or dreading being abused, while the other is thinking about or dreading not being respected as having authority. Both are creating the manifestation of abuse because of the attention given to what's being dreaded. One is dreading being abused and the other is dreading not being respected or in control. Neither may be thinking in terms of the word *abuse*, but is nevertheless creating that reality out of the fear or dread of it. But human beings are given the unique ability to survive the most threatening of situations, and this area of abuse is no different.

Overcoming abuse, whether the *abused* or the *abuser*, a person must come to the knowledge of who they are as a spiritual creative being, and this will in turn lend confidence and power to the *inner self.* When the *inner self* is validated, firmly standing in the awareness of being co-creator with Higher Intelligence—there will be no need to control anyone, or to be controlled. We are all collectively the energy of the universe, for we are the intricate aspects of God—the highest intelligence. When we understand that the nature of God resides in us, there will be no need to feel subordinate to one another, for we are all creative beings.

> *Those who abuse the world around them have already first devastated the world within themselves.*
>
> J. Meddling

Article 11

Codependences

Years ago when I served as a counselor I would speak with individuals who were challenged with moving forward after experiencing a relationship break-up. I realized how hard it was for people to move on after being committed to a relationship for so many years. Some of the women I counseled during that time found themselves attempting to hold on to men who no longer wanted to be with them. Even some of the men I spoke with could not accept the fact that they were loosing their women, and they were trying desperately to hang onto a relationship that could no longer stay afloat. I observed that people often felt the need to stay connected to the person who broke up with them. I'd often ask, "Why do you feel the need to stay connected to them when they no longer want to be with you?" The answers were usually the same: Though we are not getting alone as a couple, I still need the friendship or I need him/her to talk with because they understand me. I observed that this "connection" was related to the years of history they shared that fanned the need for staying connected. If there were children involved, it would also play a huge role in these individuals staying dependent upon one another. All of these reasons are based upon a need to feel connected to another person. Emotions are connected to all relationships no matter the dynamics of the relationship, but it is vital to being whole to emotional release a person when they no longer want to be a part of your life.

Codependency in a relationship is when the relationship becomes more important to you than you are to yourself. Codependency is when you're trying to make the relationship work with someone else who's not—it's a one-sided relationship. Sometimes these one-sided relationships can end in tragedy as we often hear about in the news. Fortunately, most codependent relationships do not end in tragedy but they do hinder people from living the full, rewarding lives they could be enjoying. Codependency becomes a serious issue when a person is unable to function in a healthy emotional and spiritual manner and/or when the inner peace of an individual is lost because of the demise of the relationship. We are social beings needing community, but we do not need to solely depend upon the existence of another in order to function in a healthy and whole manner. Of course children, the mentally challenged, and the handicap are an exception to this dependency. However, those of us who are physically and mentally independent should bear the infirmities of those who are weaker. Handicap and mentally challenged individuals are legitimately dependent upon others, but this article is addressing those who are physical and mentally whole.

Codependency exists when one fails to understand their innate divinity endowed by God—the dynamics which are only understood in one's exploration of self. We should always be on the journey of learning that we are spiritual beings endowed with greatness. This knowing of *self* gives us the confidence that our individual lives are more than the relationships that we're in. Living in the awareness of who we are as spiritual beings empowered with the greatness of God, gives us insight into the potential that lies within us. We cannot allow ourselves to fall victim to the pseudo belief that our lives lie in the hands of another. Instead, we take control of our failed relationship by moving forward with our lives. By moving forward we are then reconnecting to our *inner self* which is sometimes sacrificed when we are in a meaningful love relationship. This is why it is commonly termed "loosing yourself in a relationship."

There are many signs of codependency that are often overlooked as simply being a part of people's behavior or personalities. Some signs of codependency are:

- When a partner is self-absorbed or uninterested in a relationship where only one of them is initiating getting together or showing interest toward the other.

- When a person need someone to make a decision for them about their own life or affairs.
- When a person consistently need someone to validate their worth and value as a person.
- When a person frequently requires someone to push or encourage them in things they know they should be doing.
- When one person plays the out-of-control person, so that they get the upper hand in possessing control over the other person—thus getting respect.
- When a person depend on others to tell them what's right or wrong, or what's best for their life.
- When a person is afraid to take on new ventures alone.

There are others behaviors that could be added, but they will all stem from one basic need—the need to have someone else doing for you what you can do for yourself. God has given each of us everything that we need for our life journey. It is wired into our spiritual DNA and intertwined into our humanity. We are our own masterpiece waiting to be chiseled out of our own experiences. The life we desire is held ransom by the beliefs we hold about ourselves. We are our own devastation or our own master creation—the volume of our worth lie within the perception of our ability. We need only to look into the mirror of the *true self* and reiterate the greatness endowed upon us by God. We are the manifestation of God in earthly form, designed for greatness, endowed with divine wisdom, empowered by love, and infiltrated with independence. Our need for others is to give validation to what we internally already know about ourselves. This validation shines a light on the desires we have for our lives, and gives directions to the paths we need to take.

Article 12

Why Should
I Be Selfish

Being selfish is often looked upon as a negative thing but as we define its meaning the term can be appreciated and not be looked upon derogatively. To be selfish is to have a sense of one's self—to be connected with one's sense of need and desires, or to look inward at one's devotion to self. Being selfish is an expression of self love or self consideration. In our awareness of self we determine and make decisions for what we believe to be best for us. This sense of self is one of our internal mechanisms that provide us with the ability to survive and exist. This awareness of self is like a built-in compass—guiding and directing us in life decisions. It can also be understood as our garment of protection—for without a ***sense of self***, our insecurities and weaknesses are exposed to those who may not have our best interests at heart. Unfortunately, there are "takers" who thrive on those who are infirmed or passive. We have all probably used the expressions "I have to watch out for me" or "I'm taking care of number one" or "I'm responsible for my own self." All of these statements reflect a healthy sense of self—for this is how we survive as individuals.

Often those who lack a healthy sense of self love or self consideration are thought of as passive or weak and lacking confidence. Selfless people are often codependent—needing others to validate their worth. They often value themselves by taking the subordinate role in their relationships—an unconscious act. No matter the dynamic of the relationship—their need for being in agreement with others for fear of "rocking the boat," is the reason they put their needs last. I believe when a person continuously denounces their worth by putting others before themselves, it fester disharmony within the *inner self*. Resentment builds unconsciously towards those to whom they subject themselves, and the manifestation of self deprivation begins. Hidden hostility can turn inwardly and can lead to self destructive behavior such as overeating, bulimia, promiscuity, drug abuse, alcoholism and other disorders. It may not even be understood by the individuals why such behaviors govern their lives. This self deprivation is exhibited when a person gives more of themselves to another than what is comfortable. They may also give more love and consideration to someone else rather than to their own self. When a person continues to neglect themselves of their own needs whether those needs are material or emotional—it often causes them to feel guilty and worthless. When the giving of one's time, energy or love goes unreciprocated, the sense of *self love* diminishes. Please understand that this takes place on a very gradual scale, so I may sound a little extreme to some. But I am looking at the accumulative process.

Giving awareness to the understanding of selfishness or our sense of self preservation—grants us clarity of our innermost need and desires. We can form healthy relationships in a social environment as well as our internal personal environment, because we understand who we are and what we need to feel whole. For this reason we should not settle for what we do not want in our relationships or any other aspect of our lives that we have the power to change. There are more than enough people in the world who are in harmony with our own desires without having to settle. Settling is only resignation of the fulfillment of our needs and desires. Not being selfish and denying ourselves dilutes and extinguishes the wholeness of who we are meant to be. We only encounter frustration and anxiety in not being ourselves or the person we want to be at any particular moment. It is through our awareness of self that we acquire the objectives of our lives—breeding the confidence to trust in our own decisions and not living by the opinions of others.

Possessing self confidence also helps us in choosing the best mate for ourselves. When we are clear minded about whom we are, we will become clear about what we need from our mate and will choose someone who shares our core values. I believe that we only attract those who are in the same vibrational realm we are in. I also believe that we are what we attract, and it is through the consideration of one's self or the act of being selfish that we order our lives by allowing ourselves to be devoted to our own wishes and desires.

The act of being selfish can be a fulfilling experience when we maturely understand this concept and the empowerment that it lends to the practitioner of it. Just as the world and the cosmos have balance, so does this concept of being selfish. We will discuss this balance in Article 13 entitled **The Gift of Consideration**.

Article **13**

The Gift of
Consideration

Giving attention to one's self and being devoted to your own personal need is a healthy way to live as I discussed in the previous article **Why Should I Be Selfish**—but there is another working mechanism to this ideology. We must take into account that when we are in relationships whether monogamous or platonic, that our personal needs are often found in the giving of consideration to another's desires and wishes. For example: As an employer, I was asked by my employees for a raise and considering how much giving these raises were going to cost me, I wasn't feeling favorable towards it. But when I rethought the situation and considered how much I needed these skilled employees and how deserving they were of a raise, I had a change of heart. My personal need and desire was to maintain a smooth running business, and if it meant giving my employees a raise to heighten the moral, this is what I was going to do—and so I did. In doing so, I got ultimately what I wanted and appeased my employees at the same time. This action is what I term "The Gift of Consideration." Giving consideration to another may just turn out to be what you are unconsciously wanting for yourself. When I gave my employees what they wanted, I felt a strong sense of fulfillment. That act of consideration created a connection between me and my employees, and induced a greater loyalty between us. The moral and work productivity also increased proving to be a greater benefit to me.

Though I firmly stand on the belief of self consideration and self devotion as I mentioned in Article 12 **Why Should I Be Selfish**, I also ascribe that self love is validated when we are able to invoke this devotion of considering others. I believe that happiness is birth from a spirit of generosity, and those who give to others are expressing on a subconscious level a sense of abundance in their own lives. However, this is applicable to those who give freely from their hearts—not feeling that emotional strain when giving. I've observed that some of the most unfulfilled people in the world are those who hoard everything to themselves. As human beings, we are designed to be helpers one to another and not to merely exist alone—if we are to experience wholeness. Our ability to consider one another's needs causes us to be co-creators in the world's joy.

As co-creators of our world, we must stay connected to our cause for all of humanity in order to fulfill our purpose here on earth. We must be able to identify with the needs of the people in our lives and in our societies by willingly giving consideration to those who need it. This does not mean that we are obligated to give to everyone that ask of us, but we should live in a sense of consideration—being willing to help as seem reasonable to us. This consideration involves more than giving on a tangible level, but on an emotional, spiritual, and time plane as well.

The Gift of Consideration should be freely given as any gift is, and not for the sole purpose of reciprocity. Often people become disappointed when they give of themselves, but in their time of need, (whatever that need might be) they do not receive back what they have given out. We should never give out more than we are willing to freely give. Only give what you can afford to give away—and again I am not speaking only materialistically but in every aspect of your giving. For example, do not expect someone to love you the way you love them—do not expect a person to spend as much money on you as you spent on them, and don't expect a friend to spend as much time sympathizing with you as you spent sympathizing with them. The point is that none of us give to the same degree because our value system for how to give will differ. Do not frustrate yourselves expecting someone to be like you because none of us give of ourselves the same. Nor should we give from a sense of obligation or necessity, because this type of giving does not come from the heart. It will only leave us feeling remorseful, angry or frustrated. When we feel trapped into giving out of a sense of obligation it lends to a feeling of inner weakness. Inner weakness causes us to loose the strength of our wholeness. But when we give properly, experiencing that sense of abundance, we increase our joy, fortify our peace and restore our love for *self*. We feel best about ourselves when we give out of a spirit of gratitude. The Gift of Consideration should always feel good.

> ***When I think of the good I desire for myself and give it as an offering to another, it becomes the greatest gift of all—it becomes the Gift of Consideration.***
>
> **J. Meddling**

Article **14**

Finding Your Answers Within

Because of this modern time that we live in, with all of the internet information and the advanced internet search engines locating subjects on human growth and self awareness, people are conveniently seeking answers for their lives. While many forums of information can be found on the internet, in self help books, and in group discussions on self awareness, many fail to search for the answers to their personal lives from within. There is absolutely nothing wrong with seeking truth to grow as an individual from these forums, but we should never loose sight on our internal guidance found within ourselves.

I would dare say that most of the answers that we seek for our lives are spiritual in nature. This means that the answers are found deep within our *inner self*—our subconscious intelligence, or from our God aspect which holds all knowledge. This intelligence that possesses all knowledge is the God aspect in operation within us. This God aspect or God force within us has the answers to our relationships issues, our personal growth, our prosperity and any other questions regarding our humanity. This wisdom lies within every human being. Unfortunately, we tend to spend more time seeking answers from outsiders who may not know anymore than we do. Their personal lives might be in greater shambles than our own. And still, we're taking the advice of people who may not fully believe in the advice that they're giving. We make prayers to God as if God is somewhere out in space—not observing the truth of God dwelling within our own *being*. We look for the answers from other human beings rather than listening to the still small voice within our own hearts—the voice of our own subconscious—the voice of God. We often seek supernatural wisdom but find ourselves embracing carnal knowledge. We long for truth but often settle for a lie. However, I do believe that God uses human instrumentalities or others people to give us direction and instructions in certain situations. But our total reliance should never reside in someone else, because we are spiritual beings connected individually to the wisdom of God. We should weigh the instructions of others against our own hearts. The direction that is meant for someone else may not be the direction that the *God in you* is leading you in. The advice that they give you might be good advice and may work perfectly for them, because that is the *God in them* speaking to them. If you are considering implementing the advice and wisdom that others are sharing with you, remember that their advice and wisdom should always agree or be in harmony with your own spirit or with the God force that directs your life. As a conscious creative being, only you know what's best for you. The Bible even states a truth about us having divine knowledge or divine knowing. In 1st John 2:27 it reads: "*But the anointing which you have received of Him abides in you, and you have no need for anyone to teach you . . .* (New American Standard). Once we understand the "*Him*" in this verse as being God's knowledge abiding within us—only then can we appreciate the fact that all we need already resides within us. Therefore, when we learn to trust our own intuitions, we are learning to trust the God within us. And as we practice relying on that *knowing* within us—we're teaching our conscious mind to hear the subconscious which is the voice of God.

The unadulterated *truth* actually resides within all of us—but the problem is that we do not trust our own intuition which is the *God presence* within us. It really doesn't matter what name we give God or whether we believe God to be male or female, spirit or energy—the wisdom of God is given to everyone. But those who live in consciousness (aware of God within them) live a more purposeful filled life than those who do not. Most people believe in a God or a Higher Power, but have not learned how to connect with that Power that abides within them. This Intelligence is constantly supplying us with all the wisdom, and knowledge that we need to experience the joy of life. For human beings, it's just a matter of clearing the communication lines to hear the instructions for life clearly. Our lack of confidence in ourselves, in our decisions—disables the Intelligence of the universe from communicating clearly with us. We must believe in ourselves and in the power that resides in our human frames. So faith is a major component in allowing us to tap into the Source that's within us.

People also fail to get the answers they need because of the mentality of unworthiness they live in. If we believe ourselves to be unworthy of having the wisdom of the Universe within us—we will always be dependent on someone else to provide us with spiritual guidance. We will find ourselves relying on preachers, fortune tellers, mediums and whoever else we believe to have divine knowledge to guide us. Most people are generally taught that God responds to our faith, but if we are trusting to hear from God outside of ourselves, then we are not projecting the faith and confidence we proclaim to have. We must have confidence or "faith" that God is capable of speaking directly to our own hearts. And when God does use someone to give us instructions—it should be an acknowledgement to what we're already feeling and thinking. A *truth* presented by anyone should only confirm what is already known in the heart of the one who seeks that truth. Everyone will not be given the same exact *truth*. What's truth for one person may not be truth for another—because our experiences with life vary on multiple levels. Therefore God provides answers to us in a way that we can relate to—sometimes using our personal experiences in life to sort out *our truth*.

I often refer to God as the Higher Intelligence living within our human form because the intelligence we as humans possess is innate meaning that we're born with it. The relationship between the God of the Universe and us is that we are one. And until we gravitate to this reality—we will never understand the power and wisdom that lies within us. The wisdom and knowledge of Higher Intelligence is only as prevalent in our humanity as we are conscious of it. God indwells us, and our awareness of this presence guides us through life—making us creators of our own personal world. What we speak and believe as individual's affects the world around us, because of our creative power.

We are humans creating our own life experiences by giving our attention or energy to the thing(s) we most focus on. The answers we seek for our lives abide within us and not in another.

Let us learn to love ourselves and the *God presence* within us—creating the atmosphere to hear clearly the inaudible voice of the Intelligence of the universe. God is ever guiding us in life—but let us become quiet in our soul—hearkening to the still quiet voice speaking in our hearts. Let's find our answers—by finding God within ourselves.

Article 15

Don't Be Jealous

Jealousy is the basis of the enormous internal conflicts that we wrestle with in relationships. There are various areas in which people struggle with jealousy, and many people are not even aware that jealousy is the root of their struggles. When we feel jealous, it is a false sense that there is not enough for us, or that someone or something can be taken from us. In a relationship, it's a sense of not getting what you feel belong to you—i.e., love and affection, respect and honesty, time and attention or anything else one might consider valuable in a relationship.

Living in the mentality that the world lacks the sufficiency to supply everyone's needs including our own is a terrible misconception. The Universe, The God of Abundance is always extending the unimaginable overflow of "good" into our lives. But, no matter how much God extends this overflow, there are many who are unaware of God's provision. We must understand that Gods' provision is extended to us all, but many fail to recognize it because they do not value themselves worthy of God's provision. They fail to see their own value as an individual and they fail to see the value they hold in the eyes of the Universe. They do not understand that the Universe is actually living, breathing and abiding within them. The Universe's purpose is to supply our individual needs, and has therefore internally wired each and every human being with the ability to live a life that is fulfilling—a life of wholeness. All that we need currently exists within us—for we are complete and lack nothing. Our lives would be fulfilled if we could only grasp the reality that we are co-creators with God who abides within us—helping us create our own destinies.

Feeling jealous is the manifestation of wrong thinking that there's a lack of resources. It is however a natural emotion to feel jealousy, but we should determine that we will not be dictated by this emotion. Jealousy, like any other emotion is simply our subconscious rising to the conscious level, making us aware of our focal thoughts through our feelings. If we can gravitate to the concept that our thoughts become our realities, we will understand that absolutely nothing can be taken away from us. Understand that nobody or nothing enters or leaves our lives without our subconscious permission. Seeing that we are the creators of our own lives, nobody else can prevent us from creating the reality that we want.

If we experience being "broken up with" in a relationship we may feel jealous because we're loosing someone who rightly belonged to us—but we must understand that just as we have the right to make choices to leave or stay in relationships—so do others. Often a break-up is a sign that it's time to move on and explore new avenues of happiness. Try not to take it personal because the other person is also on a journey in their life to find their happiness. We all have the right to explore the world—and the other people in it. This would be the perfect time to ask one's self the questions—"Why I am feeling jealous and what do I perceive as being taken from me?" When you make this evaluation, incorporate the *knowing* that nothing meant for you can be taken from you except by your permission. This way of thinking will empower you to move on. There's no need for anger or revenge in these matters—even though anger might surface. If anger does come as a result of jealousy, do not try and suppress the emotion with the intention of trying not to feel it. Sometimes we must allow ourselves to feel what we feel in order to get to a better emotional state in our inner being in order to appropriately move forward. Our emotions should never be suppressed—however our actions should be tempered with harmony. It would help to take the time in evaluating the most appropriate action. We must remember that in relationships, others have a right to change their minds—and their decision might be that you will no longer be a part of their life. You might be left feeling abandon or betrayed, but unfortunately you will have to deal with the disappointment of releasing that individual from your life. We should also understand that we have no control of anyone's life but our own. When we live in the awareness that all that we encounter in life is only an experience that is added to the wholeness of our life in this earth realm—it will become an easier transition through difficult situations like these.

The harboring of jealousy will only hinder the flow of joy in our lives. Jealousy, if not handled correctly will taint ones' trust in others. We should not allow ourselves to hurt needlessly when relationships do not work out the way we want them too. We must anticipate the changes of life.

When an unwanted change such as a break-up takes place in our lives, we must understand that the *change* does not define who we are as individuals. Often we feel bad about ourselves when people walk out of our lives—or when we loose things such as houses or cars. But if we release people and things, and not focus on the situation as being a loss, we will experience human wholeness. This is the wholeness that comforts and gives us peace when all seem to be lost. The Bible speaks of this kind of comfort or peace in Philippians 4:7—"and the peace of God, which surpasses all understanding, will guard your hearts and your minds in Christ Jesus." New American Standard Bible

> *Jealously is a fear of loss—but the awareness that the Universe supplies all of our needs is the antidote. The one who focuses on loss—manifests loss into their reality.*
>
> J. Meddling

Article 16

Telling Your Body What You Want

We have heard the motto of the United Negro College Fund that says "A mind is a terrible thing to waste." There is a deep level of profoundness to this statement, because it is through our mind—or intellect and reasoning to keep it in context that we govern the activities of our reality. This reality includes the physiological as well as the spiritual aspects of our being. As co-creators with God, we have the ability to change our physical condition through the power of perception. We can make a demand on our bodies to be healthy and whole. There are other factors to this creative power that we all possess, that I will discus a little later.

Telling your body how to function is not a new theory or ideology. Ann Harrington's article on the Placebo Affect suggests that patients heal faster when they surround themselves with positive reinforcements. This is also why placebos work for so many people—when a person believes that the "sugar pill" is real medicine for their particular illness, they become better simply because they believe. The belief of becoming healthy as a result of trusting in pseudo medicine brings about the healing. This is no more than what we often relate to as mind over matter. As a person believes in their heart/mind/spirit, so it is in their reality. We can summon things into our reality with the proper perception—even when those "things" are not currently tangible. We have this incredible power to bring the unseen things into the tangible

46

realm simply by beckoning it. This belief is not only applicable to materialistic aspects but to the health of our body as well.

Living in good health in elderly years are common realities in many cultures around the world where emphasis is placed on nurturing the *inner self* or thinking in terms of being whole. The body will become healed and whole when we focus our attention on being well and not sick. How many times have we encountered other people or maybe ourselves worrying about something to the point that we became physically ill? When all of the facts about the "thing" we were worrying about was revealed, we realized that the stress was unmerited. Too often we manifest bad things into our own lives and blame the "devil" or God for being unfair to us—when all along we have not been fair to ourselves for creating that reality through our negative thoughts and verbal admissions.

In addition to creating good health through "right thinking," another applicable factor is being in harmony with our personal convictions. When we begin to create healthy bodies by correcting our thoughts and verbal admissions, we must not act in contradiction to what we know to do in proper maintenance of the body. For example, if we believe that cigarette smoking will give us lung cancer, but we continue to smoke thinking that our positive confession over our health is going to prevail, then we are having "conflicting beliefs." These belief systems will clash, and one is going to be dominant over the other. Conflicting beliefs will impose conviction or guilt in our emotional realm which will lead to negative emotions. When negative emotion set in, the creation will lean to the unwanted manifestation of bad health. On a subconscious (unknowing) level you are suspecting that the cigarette smoking is doing your body harm, so the worst shows up and your body manifest illness as a result of that belief. This is a very simple law—sometimes lost in the complexity of our rationalization. Many do not properly understand the dept that our emotions have in connection to belief. What we believe dictates our feelings and what we feel can dictate our belief—depending upon which of them becomes the dominant focus point.

To live in divine health requires living in the awareness that good health is as much spiritual as it is natural. We cannot harbor bitterness, anger, hatred, vengeance or any other negative emotion in our heart and expect to live in optimum health. Alone with harboring bad emotions, our body's metabolism, hormones, and internal functions are affected by our emotions and moods. Have you ever notice how that stressful situations will alter your ability to think clearly and to function normally? Involuntary muscles such as the intestines which are responsible for breaking down food can be affected by stress. The colon becomes sluggish and fails to properly break down the food—leading to constipation. This is because "colon motility" (the contraction of the colon muscles and the movement of its contents) is controlled by nerves, hormones, and impulses in the colon muscles. When the nerves, hormones and electrical impulses are not functioning harmoniously, physiological balances get off causing issues in the body. Stress hormones are also released into the body causing unhealthy bodily functions. It is clear to see how a good emotional state and healthy living is directly related to the proper nurturing of our *inner self* or spirit. We must be aware of our emotions at all times to assure that they are in keeping and in harmony with our desire to be healthy and whole. At this point our entire *being* will also be healthy and whole.

Think Healthy and Live Whole!

Article **17**

Marriage
Misconceptions

People seek marriage for various reasons but often fail to understand their underlining motives that lie deep within their subconscious as to why they want to be married. People usually feel that they are in love and believe that marriage will bring them the happiness or fulfillment that's missing from their lives. Mostly women marry for the sake of having that sense of security and the certainty of their mate's devotion. However, I believe that men tend to possess a sense of obligation that leads them to marriage rather than love. Now this is not to say that men are shallow and do not possess deep caring love—because we do. I just believe that men commit to marriage out of that strong sense of responsibility and loyalty that he feels towards his woman—and not the warm butterflies that his woman typically feels. Women are more emotionally connected to the whole marriage concept. What I mean by this is that women think in terms of family and nurturing at a very young age (by playing house, feeding and tending to their dolls in a nurturing manner and etc.) Young boys on the other hand have no concept of family and being a nurturer, because their main interests involve "rough housing" and battling for dominance among their young friends. But even though men and women motives for marriage might be different, there is still a need to be connected to another human being for companionship. Happiness is still found in the differences between the sexes. But the first misconception that couples usually have is thinking that marriage will fulfill their happiness. But true happiness originates from within an individual because of already possessing a sense of wholeness. No one can create your sense of well being because this is projected from your understanding of who you are. With this being said—true happiness is what every individual should be bringing into their relationship—already possessing that senses of wholeness or completeness in one's self.

Another misconception is that marriage is the "cure all" for loneliness. Some of the loneliest people I know are married. I am not by any means bashing or in opposition to marriage, but feel that most people come into marriage with expectations that are not realistic. I believe that most people do more planning for the wedding, and place more emphasis on the wedding day than they do on the relationship itself. They then hope that the grandeur of the marriage ceremony will be reflected in the marriage. Many are unconsciously thinking that all the hard work for the relationship is over after the wedding. Planning a wedding and making it beautiful has nothing to do with planning your life together. There has to be deep harmony and compatibility in order for the relationship to endure the challenges that naturally comes with being married. Marriage becoming the "cure all" is an unrealistic perception and if a person believes that marriage will make them feel whole and complete—they will once again be deceived. When people feel that sense of wholeness in the beginning of a relationship, it is usually misinterpreted feelings of excitement. This is the emotional affect of being a part of something new. This sense of wholeness and completeness that one might experiences initially in a marriage is typically short lived after the excitement and emotion wears off. When enough time has past and the sex becomes a common act of duty and the appreciation of the little charms fade away—the "real" marriage begins. Often the "business" of being a husband or wife, a mother and father, becomes the priority of the relationship instead of the maintenance of romance. The "business" of who's going to pick up the children from school, what's going to be for dinner, what bills are going to be paid this week and who's going to have time to help with the kids homework are just some of the issues that possibly stunts the romance. Though marriage is a beautiful institution, the maintenance of the family becomes the business aspect of the relationship that causes romance to sometimes fade.

Another aspect to being fulfilled relates to understanding our individuality and knowing our individual needs. Too often we expect our emotional needs to be met by our mates when actually the only person responsible for that need being met is you. People seldom get from their mates (or anyone else) what they really need emotionally—because no one at any given time truly knows what is in your heart or psyche to meet that need. Only you can know that, and is therefore your responsibility to make that place in you whole. Being emotionally fulfilled is largely based upon one's relationship with *self* and not with one's mate. Another aspect to being fulfilled is personal growth which is also spiritual growth. When our lives reflect personal growth we have become more enlightened in our perception of life. We accept the responsibility of being in control of our own emotions and behaviors when our mates do not satisfy our expectations. We will not harbor anger or regret or any ill feelings towards them when it seems that they are not contributing to our growth—because ultimately, it is not their job. This is not to say that your mate can't help or assist in you becoming all that you can be as an individual. But your individual growth is based upon your ability to mature spiritually—your ability to grow without the direct attention of others catering to you. No one can mature for you just as no one can have your personal life experiences. Your spiritual growth is watered by your personal experiences and it is a marriage misconception for you to think that your mate can spiritually mature you. Spiritual growth happens as a result of opening your mind to the unimaginable possibilities of the Universe expanding within you. However, your mate might be instrumental in helping you to become aware of the potential that lies within you if they are consciously evolved themselves.

The last marriage misconception I would like to address is the belief that just because we are both religious, there will be a mutual understanding in our spiritualality. But being religious and being spiritual are two separate ideologies. Religion can be defined as belief in God or gods to be worshipped—usually expressed in conduct and ritual or any specific system of belief, worship, etc., that often involves a code of ethics. Spirituality can be defined as the quality or fact of being spiritual, non-physical or predominantly spiritual character as shown in thought, life, etc., spiritual tendency or tone. To put it plainly, religion is a set of beliefs and rituals that claim to get a person in a right relationship with God, and spirituality is a focus on spiritual things and the spiritual world instead of physical/earthly things. We should not allow religious belief systems, which are established by people having their own agenda and interpretations of truth—dictating what is best for us as it relates to our relationships. Every relationship has its own working dynamics when the two people come into that relationship whole and mature. They will be guided by their intuition (*the inner self*) in making the right decisions for their union. This is the importance of being whole when coming into a relationship. If we obtain a sense of emotional wholeness, it is usually due to inner self growth that develops through life experiences. As human beings we are very resilient when we are challenged emotionally. We continue to thrive even through the disappointments of unfulfilled expectation which develop our sense of who we are. Our inner self and strength is fortified through our life challenges.

What marriage should be is two mature individuals understanding who they are and what they need, bringing their strengths together as a team. There should be an underlining purpose for the union if it is to endure the challenges found in every relationship. Marriage requires purpose to remain strong, because where "purpose" is not understood, failure is inevitable. Every enduring relationship has intentions or an expected goal of accomplishment. There must be a common purpose to every meaningful relationship including marriage, even as it is vital to having a meaningful goal and purpose in our individual lives.

Marriage should bring an increase of joy into your life, but if you are happy, emotionally and spiritually fulfill as a single person—then you would do well to stay single. Happiness and contentment is the best that life can offer any of us—and if you possess that as a single individual, then you are already whole as a human being. But the choice is yours and no one can own your life but you.

Be Happy And Live Well!

Article 18

The Psychology of Men and Marriage

(Why do men marry?)

I have heard women who were in long term relationships state how hard it was for them to get their men to commit to marriage. Being a man myself, it seems that we have a different prospective about marriage than women. I believe that some men see marriage as the best gift a woman can be offered, so the man saves the marriage proposal the way that women once saved their virginity. We hold out on marriage to the last minute. Men also innately have a rescue mentality—the knight and shining armor mindset to rescue the damsel who is in distress of a world filled with the ideology that there are no more committed men. So we men sometimes make that commitment to prove that we are the exceptional—and in doing that we become the knight and shinning armor.

As men, we also tend to commit to our pleasure—meaning that we will connect to the woman who is able to excite our senses and stroke our ego. Our motivation to marry is often fueled with the anticipation of being stimulated on a regular basis by the woman we believe to be the woman of our dreams. It is not always the overwhelming sense of love that we declare to have for women that lead us to matrimony. Of course a man would never confess to that. The need for constant physical, emotional, and ego stimulation is why I believe that men are more apt to marry. I also believe this to be the same motivation for a man's tendency to cheat in a relationship. Because men can always find at least a sense of fulfillment from almost any woman willing to stimulate his emotional and physical needs—even if the attention is on a temporary basis. So what marriage provide to those men who are "only" (unconsciously) looking for sexual pleasure is an allusion of guaranteed ownership to sexual fulfillment. Unfortunately it is not a realistic expectation because all relationships between men and women or otherwise will experience sexual excitement downtime. If his only goal is to be pleasured by his woman without also considering her needs, then he has not developed a mature love for this woman and is not marriage material. Neither has he come to understand the spiritual element of true love. This portrays the man who is immature and has not learned how to love and is only pleasure seeking. However, this certainly does not ascribe that all men are immature, because there are those of us who have the capacity to deeply love and care for our women. But even those of us who do deeply love our women sometimes have unrealistic expectations. Some good men who deeply love their women need their women to constantly stroke their ego. These men marry so that they can have a "mommy" figure in their life to give them the value and worth they need in order to feel whole. But this kind of man is not ready to be a husband either because his issues within himself are not resolved. He has not identified with the God source within himself that empowers him to be the confident man that a wife can confidently look up too. She will find herself spending much time in trying to grow him into the man she can emotionally and spiritually rely on. It also reveals that the little boy residing in him still desires to be the king of the hill. The little boy in him still needs the validation as a man—and this validation originates from the God source within him. Even with this flaw, he is capable of becoming a mature loving man if he is willing to expand his awareness of *self* by seeking knowledge of who he really is. But a paradigm shift has to take place within him.

The understanding of who we are as men or as human beings directly affects how we see ourselves in a relationship. We must discover who we are so that we can be whole as an individual—therefore being a whole and validated person in the relationship. We will then bring to the relationship a mature love for ourselves as well as for our mate. This mature love also brings a whole man to the marriage. When a man is as whole and complete as he can be as an individual, he will then experience true love—the love that transcends to all humanity and not only to a mate. He can be excited about marriage beyond the anticipation of sex. He can find the security he needs in one woman—because men just like women also marry for that sense of security—which is a basic human need.

As far as women are concerned (even though this article is focused on men), I believe most women tend to gravitate to the marriage concept more easily because of the mental programming that takes place in childhood—a mental programming that is unconsciously actuated in young girls. Girls at an early age view marriage in a dreamier manner whether the teaching of this view is purposeful or not. The mindset nonetheless is passed down from mother to daughter, grandmother to granddaughter or aunt to niece. Young girls witness the excitement found in conversations of marriage and the wedding dress, the ring, the flowers and so on. Because of this dreamy perception of marriage—little girls enjoy playing "House" and "Tea Time" or "Mommy & Daddy." So at an early age, this dreamy occasion is constantly festering in their subconscious—making them more prone to this desire for matrimony. We would probably not hear of a little boy wanting to play "House" with a set of dolls because boys aren't typically wired with this mindset. Instead, little boys are more drawn to "rough housing," wrestling or playing games where they are competing to being on top or in charge—being the king of the hill.

When we see the dynamics of how young boys think and play—we clearly understand why men are not automatically dreamy about marriage. For men, there is usually an element of curiosity towards the woman that drives the desire for marriage. The kind of woman who keeps us excited is the one who keep us thinking and wondering about what's coming next. As men, we are motivated towards marriage when our women bring out that boyish excitement in us whenever we are in their presence. This is the same enthusiasm we have as young boys when we are competing for being on the top—the king of the hill. Instead of being the king of the hill—the interest is now conquering the woman as to make her our prize. So when she becomes our prize, we began to want more for her than we want for ourselves. When our absence from her leaves us feeling empty or incomplete—we are in love. If a man has not reached that level of interest where he cares for his woman like he cares for himself, his love has not matured. When his care for her matures into love he will water the garden of his relationship as he projects his own inner growth. To express the kind of care for another that takes a person beyond their own comfort is the manifestation of mature love. Mature love is what brings men to the possibilities of marriage. This kind of evolved love that causes men to love another human being as much as he does himself—and not just his woman—is what I speak of in article 19 entitled **Men & Mature Love** (*In the homophobic society.*)

There are so many factors as to why each man marries. Still some marry because the sex is good with their mate or because the woman is a great cook, or because the woman shows great potential in being a good mother. Others may marry because they got their woman pregnant and wanted to do the honorable thing, while yet some feel pressured into it with an ultimatum. I would like to believe that most men do actually marry because they are in love with their women—at least this is what I've been told by 93% of the men I surveyed before writing this article.

Men Do Love, and We Love Deeply!

Men & Mature Love

(In the homophobic society)

In 2002 I moved from Nashville Tennessee to Atlanta Georgia. I became enchanted with Atlanta's beautiful skyline, and since most of my traveling to Atlanta was at night, the city always seems to be on display just for me. My work as a contracted electronic repair technician allotted me the opportunity to learn the city before actually moving there. The first place I fell in love with was Piedmont Park—being that I enjoy jogging and walking in parks. But little did I know that it was a park where lots of gays/homosexuals hung out. It is commonly known by most residences around the park that there is a designated area where gay men "hook-up." On this particular morning I went jogging at Piedmont Park when all of the sudden a guy came out and approached me with a proposition. I really didn't know that it was a proposition at first, because he spoke in a jargon that I wasn't familiar with. Because I was only interested in finishing my run, I dismissed him with the wave of a hand. But ten minutes later he showed up again on the trail, but this time blocking my path. The propositioning started once again—this time I got the message! I calmly told him that I was not gay and that I was strictly into women. But he did not want to hear that and proceeded to grab me by my arm at which time it became a bloody fight. The police and the ambulance was called for an unconscious and bleeding man—needless to say that I was the conscious one who made the call.

I had never been homophobic or even knew that term before that experience. I had to go through a whole lot of self talk as to why "I" had to experience something like that—I felt so violated even though all the man got from me was a "beat-down." At that time I wanted to hate gays and homosexuals. But I could not, because I remembered what my parents taught me about excepting people who were different from me. I remembered what I taught my own son about accepting a world that has different values and beliefs from his own—so I found myself being true to my own convictions.

In our Western society, homosexuality is not accepted as mainstream behavior—it is still frowned upon. What's unfortunate is that our society is greatly homophobic. I say unfortunate because this suggests to me that people are afraid of those who have a different sexual orientation than their own. For a person to be afraid of another's sexual orientation, indicates that they are afraid of being infringed upon or either persuaded or simply uncomfortable. So I am saying to my heterosexual brothers, if we as heterosexual men know who we are, there is no threat. When I was approached at the park, I had no concern of being changed by another's anticipation—because I knew who I was and I more confidently know who I am now. The Piedmont park encounter was a traumatic experience for me, but I yet understood that all gay people are not aggressive and inconsiderate of others preferences. I have equally as much love for my gay and lesbian brothers and sisters as I do for my strait brothers and sisters. And though I am still evolving to a better "me," I recognize my growth and maturity as I am able to show love and acceptance to all people.

When men evolve to a place of inner wholeness, our society will experience unity, peace and inner healing. Inner wholeness is the foundation, the birth place of mature love. I define mature love as loving without fear or reservation to accept, not govern by ego, not concerned about being scrutinized or criticized when helping the unpopular. Mature love embodies the belief of giving aid and comfort to the hurting without prejudice. Mature love is simply seeing and loving people the way God does—and if we want to know how God loves, just listen to our own hearts. Without mature love we as heterosexual men cannot bring social healing to our nation, communities, and families. This is not to suggest that heterosexual men (only) are responsible for making our society better in regards to accepting the differences of others sexual orientation. My objective in this article is to bring awareness to all men in taking leadership positions on making our communities a better place of acceptance—whether gay or strait. But the heterosexual community is the majority in most places, and we as the majority must be the leaders in reaching out to the minority's social groups. Not to change or persuade anyone of their sexual orientation, but to embrace one another as brothers and sisters—excepting the differences. We are not obligating ourselves to hanging-out or participating in other people lifestyles or activities just by being friendly. We can live in harmony and yet have separate lives and sexual preferences.

When a man loves maturely, he is God-connected, loving himself and possessing a healthy sense of who he is as an individual. He becomes the embodiment of God in male form, and he will serve humanity with passion and fervency. When a man loves maturely, he will water the gardens of his personal relationships with nurture and love, by giving the necessary attention to it. He never forsakes the sanctity of family. He is also able shows compassion to those of a different sexual orientation because he realizes that his son or daughter could become gay or lesbian—or better yet, born gay or lesbian. The man who loves maturely has no preference to whom he shows kindness. The Bible states *"God gives his best—the sun to warm and the rain to nourish everyone regardless: the good and bad, the nice and nasty. If all you do is love the lovable, do you expect a bonus?"* (Mathew 5: 45-46 The Message Bible). All people are regarded as precious and valued in the sight of God regardless of social status, race, education, religion or sexual orientation. I believe that all people are an expression of God.

Mature love does not choose who it will display itself to—for love is the nature of God as I stated in the beginning. God does not make a difference in providing for our human needs as we see in the Bible verse above. It does not matter to God if we are male or female, strait or gay, rich or poor, young or old, that determines God's provision. Because we are made in the image or from the spirit of God, we have the ability to love all human beings—to respond from a place of love to all humanity. When we as heterosexual men are able to love our gay and lesbian brothers and sisters—it is then evident that we are walking in wholeness and mature love. This not only applies to loving gays and lesbians but any group of people that we feel are lesser than ourselves—i.e. the homeless, prostitutes, robbers, murderers and drug dealers just to name a few. Mature love only exists when one is confident in *self,* and this *self* is not persuaded by others belief systems, convictions, or cultural norms. Mature love exemplifies the love that the Supreme God shows towards humanity—and we are the conduits of this love.

It takes a spiritually evolved heterosexual man to portray brotherly-love to another man in a public setting. Consider a situation where a brother is emotional in sharing with you some sad news—for example the loss of a parent or child, a wife leaving, or any other distressing event. I pose this question to the men of the heterosexual community, "Would you be secure enough to embrace a brother in a public place to give him comfort or encouragement knowing how our society might view two men embracing in public?" Surprisingly to me in a survey of 200 heterosexual men, 178 of them said yes. Maybe most of us would be secure enough in our manhood to show compassion in a public place in these situations mentioned. All of us can easily relate to the need of being console after loosing a loved one. But what if I change the dynamics of the story to a type of hurt that we as heterosexual men might not be able to relate too? What if that same emotionally distraught brother was all of the sudden a gay man sharing with you that his "male lover" of ten years just passed away, or that his "male lover" walked out of the relationship—what would be the response? I am giving this scenario to bring awareness to the mentality of men when the situation of another brother hurting might seem unmerited. Often we as heterosexual men feel that if another brother's hurt is something that we cannot personally relate to (as in the case of the guy whose male lover walked out) we may not be sympathetic. Can we still walk in mature love towards those whose hurts are different from ours or whose pain we cannot personally relate too? When we see through the eyes of God and love through God's spirit, we only see the one who is hurting as an opportunity to show compassion. At times like this, we have the opportunity to serve as the comforting hand of God.

In some African societies even today as an expression of friendship or honor towards a person—two men holding hands while walking down the streets is common. When I was in South Korea in August 2010, I saw many business men walking and holding one another hands as an expression of friendship. Sometimes they even held hands in groups of five while on their way to lunch. Because our Western society has such a misconception of masculinity, our heterosexual men suffer with male identity issues. Heterosexual men who do not understand what it means to be masculine are sometimes seen acting "hard" or macho—giving the impression to their young sons and other young boys who are observing the behavior that this is what it means to be a man. In actuality it is only teaching them how to look like a secure man on the outside but not actually being one. These young boys are only learning how to hide their compassion and to mask their insecurities. Many of these young boys come into manhood never learning how to verbalize their feeling of hurt or anger—so they act-out as wounded misguided soldiers, devastating anyone who do not subject to their masquerade of insecurity.

When a man's love is mature the opinions of others does not prevent him from expressing this brotherly-love by doing good deeds towards his fellow-man. Mature, God-like love is displayed by providing for the needs of another and should not be subjected to ridicule or discrimination—nor should the one expressing this love be accosted by prejudice. Too often people judge what they see as being right or wrong based on their own personal opinion, biases or prejudice. To live in the love of the Supreme God, we as heterosexual men must forsake the fears and insecurities imposed upon us by our society and live as mature and loving beings.

As mature men, let us walk as confident representatives of the Supreme God—understanding that we are the offspring's of something or someone much bigger than our societies expectations.

Article 20

Homosexuals . . . ,
Born or Made?

A frequently asked question concerning homosexuals—"Are they born or made?" What determines sexual orientation? What makes a person gay, lesbian, bisexual, or straight? These sort of questions hold an undeniable interest to people in general and the answers are still hotly debated both by the experts in the field and by society at large. I interviewed and surveyed gay men and women about how or what introduced them to same sex relationships. I heard a variety of stories that revealed to me the many dynamics of same sex relationships. However, I do not have a conclusive answer but I do hold the opinion that gays and lesbians are a combination of being self-made by way of choosing, born into it by way of genetics, or experienced some form of sexual violation at a young age that traumatized and confused their sexual identity that led them into same sex relationships. In this article, I will share the information that I found in case studies that give validity to my opinion. I will also express my personal thoughts on the matter and share some stories given to me by homosexuals who identities are protected with fictitious names.

Wikipedia has an article entitled Biology and Sexual Orientation. This study deals with the research into the role of biology in the development of human sexual orientation. It is also stated that no simple, single cause for sexual orientation has been conclusively demonstrated. But research suggests that it is by a combination of genetic, hormonal, and environmental influences, with biological factors involving a complex interplay of genetic factors and the early uterine environment. Biological factors which may be related to the development of a heterosexual, homosexual, bisexual or asexual orientation include genes, prenatal hormones, and brain structure.

The majority of us have experienced sexual attraction toward another person, and when attraction is present it influences our behavior, mood, social interactions, and influences the image that we have of ourselves. Since this plays such a key role in our perception of *self*, it is only natural that we would be interested in knowing about its origins, and why we are oriented only toward people with certain characteristics and not others. Cristian C. Bodo in his August 7, 2007 article, Biology and Sexual Orientation states: "Whether sexual orientation is the result of a conscious choice by the individual, as opposed to just another trait that comes "built-in" in our system—helps determine if it should be categorized as a moral problem or not. This seems to matter a lot in shaping out attitudes toward sexual minorities. Specifically (and for better or worse), the public appears to be more sympathetic to variations from the norm—in this case strict heterosexuality, if they are convinced that the individual has no authoritative opinion on this departure since it is the product of biological determination. On the other hand, sexual minorities have traditionally regarded this argument with suspicion. They fear that scientific research may open the door to treating these variations as little more than a disease and those efforts will be made to reduce or eliminate incidences of homosexuality in human populations." What I personally gather from Cristian Bodo statement is: In order for society to deem homosexuality as a moral issue, we must first determine the cause. What we believe about this matter will determine our attitudes towards people who are of different sexual orientation. People may be more sympathetic towards homosexuals if they view them as someone who has a disease or imbalance—not being able to control their preference. However, the sexual minority would not want to be viewed as being "sick"—and who would? The minority in this matter would be treated as diseased individuals—being made to feel as if they are a lesser person or someone who is infirmed with an illness—when they consider themselves as whole as the next person.

An experiment was done on male lab rats by castrating them at birth that showed that they no longer showed interest in the female rats after being castrated. The sexual drive for the male rats is induced by the testosterone hormones found in the testes. When the female rats were injected with the male hormone (testosterone) early in life, they later showed an attraction to other female rats. These experiments helped in the determination of sexual orientation. If homosexual tendencies are proven to be a disease or hormonal imbalance as we see in the experiment with the rats, how is it that we judge it as an immoral problem? As a society that frowns on illegal drug use, do we judge a new-born as immoral when they are born drug dependent because of a mother's addiction to drugs? How can the heterosexual society place judgment or deem those who are genetically or who are hormonally wired differently from us as being immoral.

Sexual abuse is another factor that could be responsible for homosexuality. It is a well-documented fact that many homosexuals were sexually abused when young. The Associated Press noted in late 1998 that according to an analysis of 166 studies covering the years 1985-1997 as many as one in five boys were sexually abused. It also concluded that sexual abuse of boys is underreported and undertreated. It was also reported by a nationwide news media in May 2013 that numerous men in the military who are heterosexual, came forward and reported that they had been raped by other men in their unit. This act went unreported for years and is just now coming to surface.

Earlier studies have shown that 25 percent to 35 percent of girls are sexually abused. If sexual abuse happens to a child that is one or two years old, he or she may not remember it later in life because it happened at such a young age. However, the trauma can still govern the psyche and affect the rest of the victim's life. Some homosexuals will protest that they were never sexually abused, but if it happened in those earlier years that I spoke of, they might not have a way of consciously remembering a violation.

However, there is another school of thought on homosexuals "not" being born with the same sex orientation. The organization H.O.M.E. (Heterosexuals Organized for a Moral Environment) states: "That there is currently no definitive proof that anyone is born homosexual. Several studies by homosexual researchers claimed to find some possible biological bases for homosexuality. But other scientists easily pointed out the flaws in those studies, and the results of those studies have yet to be replicated by others. In the words of pro-homosexual *Newsweek* magazine: "In the early 1990s, three highly publicized studies seemed to suggest that homosexuality's roots were genetic. More than five years later the data have never been replicated." This fact has been almost totally ignored by the biased, untrustworthy, dominant liberal media. And in the May/June 2008 issue of *Psychology Today* stated: "No one has yet identified a particular gay gene. There is no all-inclusive explanation for the variation in sexual orientation, at least none supported by actual evidence. There are many different mechanisms involving both nature and nurture, not a single one, for producing homosexuality." This school of thought also believe that homosexuals were born heterosexual but experienced some type of sexual trauma that confused their sexual orientation. They also believe that homosexuals can be reconverted to their proper orientation. This school of thought believes those who oppose using therapy to change homosexuals into heterosexuals are, in effect, trying to keep homosexuals locked into homosexuality. Those who oppose such therapy do not want homosexuals to have a choice—a way out of homosexuality. That is un-American, inhumane, intolerant, and meanly oppressive—argued by the organization H.O.M.E. Heterosexuals Organized for a Moral Environment."

However, I personally believe that there are those who are born with homosexual tendencies because I have encountered one and two year olds who mannerism was opposite of their gender. Before these children were of age to know anything about sexuality, they were portraying uncharacteristic behavior of their gender. If detected early by the child's behavior or genetic testing for dominant genes or hormone imbalances, can these children be treated with proper counseling or hormone injections? I do not know—but what I do know is that no matter the person's sexual orientation, our basic human needs still remain the same. We all need love and respect, validation and security. The fundamentals of humanity should never be denied anyone based upon one's religion, beliefs, social status, race, education or sexual orientation. I also believe that those who are prejudice against gays and lesbians are no different from some of the whites from slavery through the 50s and 60s who despised, hated, degraded, and fault against blacks having rights. We are not a black race or a white race, nor are we a homosexual or heterosexual race—we are simply the human race. We are simple individuals either trying to find or make our way through life with as little conflict as possible. But no gay or lesbian (or any person) should ever be subjected to conform to a society that denounces their individuality for the mere comfort of the popular norms. All of us have a right to be who we are!

> *We hold these truths to be self-evident, that all men are created equal, that they are endowed by their Creator with certain unalienable Rights, that among these are Life, Liberty and the pursuit of Happiness.*
> **U.S. Declaration of Independence**

Same Sex Relationship Dynamics

These stories reflect some of the relationship dynamics that I mentioned at the beginning of this article and how some were introduced to homosexuality. There names have been changed to protect their identity.

Bob, a gay man, age 36 tells his story of how when he was 9 years old was taken into a church closet by his Sunday school teacher on a Saturday evening after a church event and was molested. He was told by this adult that if he told anyone, that the same would be done to his younger brother who was only 6 years old at the time. To protect his younger brother, Bob kept quiet about the matter for two years—the entire period that this violation went on. Bob expressed to me that he had never had any desires for boys before this experience—in fact he had a girlfriend when all of this first happened. When he turned fourteen, Bob had his first voluntary sexually encounter with a male who was four years older than him in which he initiated the relationship. From that point on Bob was seeking out men for companionship even though he is still attracted to women and dates them. Because of social pressures and family, he had to keep his sexual orientation a secret, so he masked it by marrying a woman that he was really in love with. That marriage only lasted three years. Bob's wife divorced him—thinking that he was cheating on her with another woman when all along he was cheating with a man.

Sylvia a 26 year old lesbian had her first sexual encounter with a girl when she was only eight. Sylvia always knew that she liked girls preferably to boys. She stated that she remembers kissing other little girls on the lips around the age of 4 years old and would get spankings regularly for it. She did however date and have sex with men but found it uncomfortable and unsatisfying. Sylvia says that she has never been sexually violated but has always had a desire for women.

Lou, a 40 year old male/transvestite who was molested by two of his uncles from the age twelve to seventeen enjoys sex with both men and women. Lou prefers sex with women more than men, but likes to dress as a woman when "picking up" women. Lou stated that his uncles chose to molest him and not his two younger brothers because he/Lou enticed his two uncles. Lou's two younger brothers had very feminine characteristics, and Lou was the masculine of the three, but it was Lou who considered himself "freaky" as he called it. His brothers have never been in any same sex practices, and furthermore both of Lou's brothers became the "ladies man" when they reached their early twenties. These same brothers are both in successful marriages and feel that Lou's lifestyle as a transvestite is repulsive.

Cindy is a very attractive 32 year old woman with two young boys. She was introduced to lesbianism out of a game of "dare" at the age of eighteen. She states that she was only curious about making love to another woman but wasn't particularly attracted to women sexually. After several years of "only satisfying her curiosity" as she stated—became hooked on having sex with women. I asked Cindy, "What is it that hooked you into this practice?" She told me that it just felt more natural being with women than men. But Cindy stated that when she wants to feel safe and protected she prefer the company of a man. Cindy only allows her sons to see her with her male companions, because she feels that this is the more healthy perspective of a family. Nevertheless, she states that "I must have my girlfriends on the side, and I will never marry a man."

Terrance and David are two middle age homosexual men, who had both been married to women in their past lives. Currently they are living as gay lovers on the "down low" or the "DL" as it is so commonly called. This couple have been in a relationship and living together for more than twelve years, but state that they will never get married. They stated, "Marriage between two people of the same sex is an abomination to God, but cohabitating is acceptable." While other gay unions are fighting for marital rights, Terrance and David totally reject the idea and live their lives quietly and discrete.

We can clearly see the many spectrums of perceptions in the same sex relationships. What I have learned is that people have a variety of sexual appetites and tendencies that is too complex to judge. I do not know who possess the authority to deem homosexuality an immoral act or "sin"—or is it even a moral/ sinful issue at all. Could it simply be that this is just another God—given choice or experience to this thing we call life?

Just as children are born into the world with deformities, couldn't homosexuals also be born with sexual tendencies that they are pre-exposed to genetically? Some religious people might say that God cannot make a mistake that would cause them to be homosexual or lesbian—but isn't it strange that when a child is born with one arm or no legs, that we do not challenge God on an error made? If we believe that God allows some children to be born with (what we perceive as human beings—seeing that we have limited knowledge) a handicap—who can say that homosexuals are not in the same category? Who can deem that any so-called birth deformity is a mistake? Since we are human beings with limited understanding and insight, we cannot completely know what is the mind or intention of God. Therefore, we cannot rightly judge a birth defect, whether it is physical or genetically as an error or mistake. Neither should we proclaim to know the path that any life should take except our own.

Though I truly believe human beings to be God incarnated, I am also persuaded in my own heart that our humanity sometimes prevents us from understanding issues like this clearly. Therefore let us not seek an occasion to be offended of others sexual orientations. Our *higher self*—where I believe God dwells within us, leads us as human beings to not judge this matter, and these individual situations from our human perspective—but to simply show compassion and love to all mankind as our main objective.

Let us only be concerned about loving and healing the spirit of humanity by allowing every individual to have their own life experiences—understanding that we are not the determiner of the paths others choose to take.

Article **21**

Married . . . ,
But Attracted to Someone Else?

In a world where things and situations are so imperfect, it is somewhat humorous to me that people look for perfection in marriage. Most people definition or understanding about what a perfect relationship consist of is unrealistic. Many perceive that marriage is to be without personal conflicts and that they will never have to struggle with old or new attractions. This is where I believe the first mistake is made. Failure in understanding that there will always be distractions (other people that you're physically attracted too) is one of the gravest mistakes made particularly by young couples. As human beings who innately desire new experiences and new adventures, we will meet other people while in a relationship that will also attract our attention. It does not mean that we have intentions to be unfaithful, but shows that we are curious creatures attracted to variety. Many who are married have experienced long-term love relationships before meeting their mate. But emotional ties can still exist even after people have broken up. These emotional ties do not necessarily go away just because you are in a relationship with someone new. Instead these ties can lie dormant in the realm of our emotions—sometimes undetected until later. With certainty, people can and do bring these unresolved hidden emotions into a marriage—many times unaware.

Undetected and unresolved past love relationships often do not show up until problems arise in the current relationship. It is when things go wrong in the current relationship like the lack of attention or lack of attraction to name a couple, that reminiscence of the former relationships creeps in. Sometimes in marriage it is simply boredom or lifestyle complacency that brings the reminiscing—not particularly conflict between the two people themselves. This is why I believe that people can "re-fall" in love and find themselves attracted to people from their past while being married. People enjoy new relationships because it feels good when you have that special connection with someone. But often in marriage, life between the two people become complacent and predictable and the marriage goes down the long unwanted road of boredom. Many people in this marriage situation began to seek out someone to share some fun-time with—and not necessarily with the intention to cheat. Sometimes it's a past lover or someone new—often people seek anyone who can bring that excitement back into their life. Once the excitement is found with the other person, feelings naturally began to deepen for that person. Unfortunately, the heart of the married person no longer belongs to their spouse, but to the new person or the old ex. This dichotomy happen more often in relationships than what many would confess to. However, I am not advocating that anyone would go outside their marriage or monogamous relationship just because they get bored or become unsatisfied. Neither am I advocating that people allow past ex's to come back into their lives when they are in a current relationship—but it does happen and people do get carried away by their feelings. There are many people who are married wishing they could be with the one that they truly feel connected to, but remain faithful and loving to the one that they are with. Like the song Luther Vandross sang, "*If you can't be with the one you love, then love the one that you're with.*" Lots of people are doing it everyday!

Most of us are not living a fairy tale relationship, but our relationships can possess excitement and adventure. Create the adventure in your relationship by first appreciating the person that you have. By showing your mate that you appreciate them, you will nurture to life the creativity and bliss that you thought was lost. We only need to possess a realistic view of our humanity, and understand that Higher Intelligence is always guiding us into optimum maturity.

Love yourself . . . love the one you are with . . . and watch your relationship grow into a masterpiece.

Article 22

Do Opposites Attract?

People have frequently asked me when speaking of relationships "Do opposites attract?" The word "attract" mean: to draw to itself or oneself, to make approach or adhere to, according to Webster New World Dictionary. In a relationship, to attract is the same which mean to *draw to one's self, to adhere to,*—but I would like to add that it also mean *to be in harmony with or connected to.* If we can focus on the definition *to be in harmony with,* I believe that it will lend us the clearest understanding of "attraction" as it relates to relationships.

When we are in harmony with another person we feel a sense of connection—a sense of oneness or a feeling of agreement. We have heard the saying "birds of a feather flock together." This saying stems from a belief that people tend to associate or *draw to, adhere to,* or *be in harmony with* those who are like themselves. Humans connect and disconnect on subconscious levels. One example of this is when we meet people for the first time, we often sense a "like" or "dislike" a connection or disconnection with that person. Often we are unaware on a conscious level that we are not in harmony with other people. But this feeling of disconnect that we experience is our inner *self* discerning the energy/spirit of the other person. If our energies conflicts with someone else's then we say things such as "I don't know why I don't like them" or "my spirit does not agree with them," or "I'm not feeling them." When our energy is in harmony with theirs, then we might say things such as, "I feel like I've known them all my life," or

72

"I'm really feeling them" or "we have a kindred spirit." All of these expressions signify that we are experiencing harmony or disharmony with the people that we meet on a subconscious level. At times these feelings that we have about people that stem from our subconscious is recognized later at our conscious level. We then make statements such as "I've never liked them from the moment I met them" or "I clicked with them the very first time we met."

So when we attract, we are simply sharing harmonious energy with those who are akin to what we desire. Even in the innermost aspect of our being where our deepest desires and wishes abide—we attract those who are in vibrational connection with those desires. An example of this is when the quiet conservative man finds himself drawn to a boisterous outgoing woman. He is drawn to the outgoing woman because on a subconscious level, she fulfills his inability to be more outgoing or expressive. Sometimes people fear or are shy about expressing their real self. Usually this person does not want to have a lot of attention drawn to them but deep down inside they have a need to be noticed and admonished. On the other hand they may fear the rejection of others if they were to allow their true colors to show. So they live vicariously through the lives of the people they bring into their circle, and they draw to themselves those who express that part of their *inner* self that is inhibited. I believe this to be the reason for people having what I call *self conflicting personalities*. This is when a person expresses their inhibited personality in private, versus the personality they project to the public. The *self conflicting personality* is when the person feels and acts one way privately but feel and acts differently when in the presence of those that they feel might condemn or scowl at their behavior. This inner conflict becomes the challenge that people have in attempting to be who they really are at all time. As a resolve to the issue people tend to find or attract someone they can vicariously live the inhibited aspect of their personalities through.

Sometimes we attract people into our lives that reflect our inhibited "dark side"—the part of our self that is secretive from the world. There are other factors and variables as to why we attract things, people and situations into our lives that we do not want, such as bad relationships and all types of abuses.

Why would the *abused* attract an *abuser* into their life? This is a good question to ask, because most people would not purposely invite someone into their life who is abusive. Unfortunately, most people invite things into their lives by default (by way of subconscious attraction) that is emotionally and spiritually toxic to them. Read article 10 **Overcoming Abuses**.

Ultimately we draw or attract those who are in synergy with us. The subconscious attraction we mentioned a moment ago derives from the core of our being. This is the same energy that we display to the world as confidence or weakness, joyfulness or sadness, wholeness or neediness, love or hate. Whatever we as individuals display to the world by way of our energy, (that we are unconscious of) will be the same magnetism whereby we attract. One who focuses on their abuse, pain, anger, or joys, pleasures, and happiness will attract into their life those very things. We must anticipate meeting those who are emotionally and spiritually healthy for us and those healthy relationships will become our reality as long as we remain focus. The same is true when we anticipate or expect negative people or situations to show up in our lives—they also manifest. The one who spends energy worrying about getting an abuser will usually end up with a person who is abusive, because we attract what we give the most attention and energy to.

We can only attract that which resonates from within us. We have been given by Higher Intelligence the ability to summon the unseen to the seen, the intangible to the tangible, and the supernatural to the natural. All of us possess the creative ability to form our inner world to our liking by changing out perception. And when we change our perception of the things around us—the things around us manifests according to our will.

Article **23**

Why People Cheat
In Relationships

Both male and female share the same basic need in relationships and when these needs are not met, some people tend to search for a sense of fulfillment elsewhere. In surveying 100 men and women who had cheated in past relationships, 85% did not set out to be cheaters—they were only interested in having a new experience with a new person that did not involve having sex. But when the lack of attention in one capacity or another goes unfulfilled infidelity issues can creep in. Three key points I would like to make before I go any farther are:

1. People do not always cheat just to get extra sex on the side.
2. Just because a person cheats once does not mean that they are always going to cheat.
3. Anyone who is unfulfilled in a relationship will cheat.

Depending on ones' *inner constitution* or personal *convictions*, cheating may never occur during the relationship regardless of personal dissatisfaction in a relationship. So these can all be misconceptions. I will go back to each one of these three points in detail. I would like to express my opinion of what's needed in every healthy relationship in order to prevent the potential deterioration that leads to infidelity.

As I mentioned earlier, that males and females have the same basic need in relationships. The first fundamental element to a healthy relationship is respected. To feel respected is to have a sense of honor and value bestowed upon you—this is how the ego in every person is stimulated. The ego or *ones' image of self* is what primarily makes us who we are in relationships, and in every other aspect of our life. When we feel devalued by our mate, it will sever the cord of romance and destroy sexual attraction as well as any other attraction that we have towards our partner. Even in the midst of disagreements, respecting your mate's feelings and showing sensitivity will fortify the relationship bond. But if you do the opposite and call your mate out of their name during a disagreement, you will weaken if not destroy the relationship bond. The people we love must feel valued at all times—and all the more when there is friction between us. This is why name calling should be eliminated in arguments—because once you destroy your partners' *image of self*—respect becomes voided. It is so hard to restore a persons' image of self after shattering them with a degrading remark. Even when an apology is later given, a person may still remain wounded. Reconciliation on the *soul* level is not easily made once a person is wounded.

The next fundamental element of a healthy relationship as it relates to *self image* is telling your mate how attracted you are to them. Every ones' body changes over time and none of us are going to remain in our twenty year old bodies. It is so crucial that we continue to admire and regularly flirt with our mates. People like to know that they are still appealing in the eyes of their lover—and even to others. This is why I believe that being harmlessly flirted with (flirting without any intentions) is healthy for a persons' self image and ego. When you deny your mate the attention that they deserve by not flirting with them or paying them the attention they deserve—it can become the reason for them stepping out in the relationship. This is not to say that we are solely responsible if our mate cheats on us if we do not give them enough attention, but we can at best do our part in securing our mates egos.

In referenced to misconception number one (1)—People do not always cheat just to get extra sex on the side: Often it is a matter of getting attention from others who build their self image and make them feel good about themselves. As I stated earlier, sometimes it is simply the attention that is not being received from home. No matter how long you have been with your mate they need to hear you say, "*You still turn me on*"—and it should not only be said when sex is wanted (referring to the guys). If you do not remind your mate of how attracted you are to them, someone else will certainly express their attraction to your mate. This is such a major component because our sexuality and sensuality is intertwined with our image of self.

Misconception numbers two (2)—"Once a cheater always a cheater" is another misconception. People cheat for so many reasons. Some cheatings are premeditated and yet others are encountered by a compromising situation. It makes no difference as to how one is trapped into a web of infidelity—cheating is not necessarily a compulsion for everyone. Some "step-out" because of lack of personal attention given by a mate as I mentioned earlier, but also to get even with a cheating partner—in which I've never understood since the objective in cheating is not to get caught. So I do not understand how one is getting "even" if the other is not suppose to know about it? Still, others may become temporarily bored sexually with their partner or may need validation in regards to feeling attractive and "still having it." Others may simply "step-out" by mere curiosity of being with someone new. No matter the reason, it does not mean that a person is going to do it again. How many of us have experimented with drugs, alcohol, or gambled away a paycheck, and only tried it once or maybe even a few times, but never went back to it afterwards? Sex is no different! Human beings are highly sexually driven creatures—coupled with curiosity. But I would be remiss to add that once a person cheats and gets away with it, it becomes easier to do it again. The human dynamics of having adventure in one's life—even at the potential risk of hurting another is a real factor.

For some people, their *image of self* or ego is directly connected to their sexual abilities. What I mean is that some people's (particularly men but not exclusively) value is in their ability to be a good lover so they take on every sexual encounter they can find (having affairs) to prove themselves to be the best. This is behavior describing the man who is still seeking to be the little boy who still want to be the "king of the hill," as I stated in article 18 **The Psychology of Men and Marriage**

(*Why do men marry*). Or the woman who is still a little girl on the inside seeking the approval of a father. So she frequently engages in affairs to gain that attention that she missed from a father that she never gained the approval of. For these people, their sexuality defines their self worth in the relationship—and as unnerving as it may be infidelity becomes common place for people with these mindsets. Unfortunately, cheating is part of the complexity of many relationships issues. I am by no means condoning or advocating cheating in any relationship for any cause. I believe that there is enough relationship diversity in the world today to not have to cheat, i.e., "swingers." Swingers are those couples who invite other couples or individuals into their bedroom—giving themselves sexual diversities. If you are a person who like having sex with multiple partners but yet feel the need to have one person that you're committed to in a relationship—this lifestyle is for you. Find a mate who also believes in "swinging," and do not violate the sanctity of a relationship with someone who believes in monogamy.

From years of observing human behavior—especially around religious groups, I have learned that human nature will always rise no matter what spiritual or religious title one carries. I have had parishioners to tell me in confidentiality that had it not been for a "fleeting affair," that they would not have had the fortitude during their discord in their marriage to endure those tough times—and that they would have ended up in divorce. These parishioners both men and women have been married for many years now and are yet with their spouses, but stated that they have never had an affair since. Once again, I am not advocating infidelity in any situation, and by no means making light of this potentially hurting act, but simply stating that cheating is prevalent. It is simply the unfortunate reality of human behavior in many relationships.

Let's look at misconception number three (3)—Anyone who is unfulfilled in a relationship will cheat: Even though most people become unfaithful because of lack of fulfillment (in whatever area of the relationship), it doesn't necessarily mean that they will cheat. Some people have very strong convictions about remaining loyal and faithful in relationships. Some are faithful and loyal even to the point of totally sacrificing their on happiness to remain true to their mate.

These people live in a heighten awareness of observing personal morals and high values. Their ego or *image of self* is often defined and validated by their ability to maintain a clean and clear conscious—which is admirable. Living in a mindset of self respect and self honor is their mission. The comfort that they find in remaining faithful in an unfulfilling relationship, gives them their inner contentment towards the relationship. This inner contentment lends to their self confidence, and they find solace in living with integrity. Needless to say, that they observe a high constitution and are a rare breed.

Lack of fulfillment does not equal a cheating mate, but in our relationships, we should always do our best to be the best mate we can be. We should always consider the needs of our partner as we consider our own. Give to your partner the love and attention that you would give to yourself. Your partner will hopefully see your efforts and reciprocate that same affection.

Article 24

Oatmeal Sex . . . B-o-r-i-n-g!

From years of serving as a counselor I have observed that many problems in relationship are issues with sex. Probably more vocalized by men, because men are more focused on seeking physical pleasure as I earlier stated in article 18 **The Psychology of Men and Marriage** (*Why do men marry*). In my experience with counseling women—they tend not to comment negatively on the performance of their men if they are pleased with the way they are being treated overall by their men neglect to secure their women and possess the mindset that "it's all about me" in the bedroom—which adds to a woman's sexual satisfaction. But if men neglect to secure their women and have the mindset that "it's all about in me" in the bedroom—the woman is going to feel neglected. Women might not share with me in a counseling session about their dissatisfaction with their men, but you better believe that she is sharing it with her girlfriends. She will be very expressive about his bedroom shortcomings when she is in the privacy of her "girls." Nevertheless, sex always becomes a concern at different times in every relationship—no matter the orientation of the relationship.

Sex is to be enjoyed by both parties, and this act of expression needs a little variety every now and then. Some men and women feel that the mere act of having sex with their mate is enough to sustain the satisfaction—but that is one of the biggest misconceptions of all. I believe that variety is indeed the spice of life. A change in position, experimenting in various places, and even a little role playing might be necessary every once in a while to keep the lovemaking experience fresh and new. Ignore the bedroom creativity—and you will end up with "oatmeal sex." Oatmeal sex is boring sex—the worse kind of all, because it lends to bedroom complacency. The relation I am making between oatmeal and sex is that you can eat oatmeal every day for the remainder of your life, and it will nutritionally supply your need—but how starved would your taste buds be? Well, the same is true about boring sex—it might knock the sexual edge off, but how dissatisfied will your sexual taste buds be?

Many people are starving for the ecstasy that should be found in their sex life. Their sexual experience is just enough to knock that sexual edge off but not enough to satisfy the deep longing for true sexual connection. Many couples rely on their partners to tell them that a change is needed in the bedroom. Often, the concern of hurting the partners' feelings prevents this needed communication from happening. In order for sex to become "lovemaking," an understanding of what's needed or expected must be expressed—mingled with sensitivity. Unless the partner knows what is needed or wanted, no change will take place. If it is believed that magically everything will naturally work itself out, then you are fooling yourself—and you will continue to experience the "oatmeal sex." When this kind of complacency sets in, people can be tempted to cheat and become unfaithful. Not because they have fallen out of love but because they have fallen out of excitement with their mate. If *physical* cheating does not become an issue, usually men will turn to pornography, while women turn to online flirting or on the job flirting and etc., because women need that mental stimulation in order to feel attractive. However, both man and woman might turn to masturbation as their primary source of sexual relief. Of course there are various ways people find sexual pleasure beyond what I have mentioned!

In regard to a person's *needs being met*—many women cannot achieve orgasms with men unless they (women) play an active part in touching themselves during intercourse. If the men are uncomfortable with their women stimulating themselves during intercourse to achieve an orgasm, then women usually turn to their "toys" in their private time. Still, some women must have oral sex in order to experience an orgasm—so her man has to diversify his sexual game if he aims to please her.

In order for sex to turn to "lovemaking," couples must respect each others needs and not be judgmental of their partner's sexual cravings. Just as people have different food preferences they also have different sexual preferences. Your partner should not be judged as immoral just because they enjoy "kinky sex," and you prefer conservative sex. One who likes bananas is no more moral or immoral as the person who likes peaches. There is absolutely no difference in sexual preferences. However, I do believe that it is vitally important to discuss the matters of sex and sexuality before engaging into a relationship. You might save yourself a whole lot of disappointment in the bedroom when you know up-front what the other need and expects. On the other hand, no matter how much discussion is made on the sex issue, some things you will have to learn along the way. Peoples' appetites for sex change in relationships even as our appetites for foods changes as we go through phases in our life. We are ever growing and ever changing beings in every capacity of our humanity—including our sex lives.

Article 25

A Relationship Issue
(My Friends are My Friends)

How many times have we heard of couples getting into arguments about one another's friends, or complaints about how the other spend too much time hanging out with old friends. Some of these old friends may consist of former boyfriends or girlfriends. This is an age old feud that we hear about in almost every couple's relationship at one time or another. Should we discard ex-boyfriends or girlfriends when we come into new relationships?

First we must look at the two individuals coming into the relationship. It is important that we understand who we are as individuals. If a person knows that they have the propensity to be excessively jealous—they should consider finding a mate who has that same quality of wanting exclusivity rights. This means finding someone who is compatible with them in that regard, and who understands the challenge of sharing their mate's time with someone else. I believe that compatibility (essence of mutuality) is crucial to the survival of any relationship. We cannot change people because we are not able to change the experiences of their lives that have shaped them into who they are. The person who has the propensity to be excessively jealous may have experienced a heart-break due to an unfaithful partner that has led them to a point of not being able to trust. That person then need to find someone who shares the same sentiment and the two can grow together in their areas of weakness. This not only relate to jealousy but any issue of where differences and expectations might collide in a relationship. In order for a relationship to develop properly there has to be a foundation of compatibility that consists of mutuality and understanding one another weaknesses.

However, we must understand that in relationships there is nothing wrong with having old friends who might be exes—if the exes are strictly platonic friends. However, there should be a mutual agreement with a mate about how much time can be spent with this friend—because an open dialogue will creates trust in the relationship. Also, there should be an understanding between the two that a real friend will never jeopardize your relationship, and if an old friend attempt to do otherwise—it would be to the best interest of your relationship to sever the closeness of that friendship. That has to be the ground rules established between couples. But there are people in our lives who have significantly influenced us into being the person we are today. Some of these friends are our mentors, role models and confidants—and they are anchors in our lives. And then there are those to whom we have deep emotional connections to (not speaking of romantic ties) that are vital to our emotional support system. These friends are the one's that if we fell out of touch with them because they moved far away or they simply died—we would make the emotional adjustment but their absences would always be felt. There would be a longing for this kind of friend to whom you feel a "soul tie" or spiritual connection to. So maintaining a friendship with a friend like this should be encouraged—because this kind of friend truly has your best interest at heart and would never violate your relationship with your mate.

But there is one thing that we must understand and that is, "my best friend" is not obligated to become my mate's best friend—and vise versa. Higher Intelligence has given all of us friends and relationships individually. We should not allow ourselves to become angry when our mate is not interested in making their best friend ours. I also believe that our mates should be made aware of our close friends in the beginning of a relationship to discard any confusion. And yet, I believe that every one of us need someone to confide in—someone we trust to vent frustrations and disappointments with outside of our romantic relationship when life becomes challenging. A good friend will only enhance our emotional quality—making us a better person in our love relationship. But my friend is indeed my friend and should not be forced to become a friend to my mate. Only by mutual consent should our friends become associated with our mate, because the compatibility that one has with their friend may not be as harmonious with their mate.

We should not be obligated to forsake meaningful and healthy relationships with old friends. Our first obligation should be to our own wholeness—therefore it would be unwise to pursue relationships with those who would pull us away from those who lend to our sense of wellbeing. It behooves us to seek true compatibility (the essence of mutuality) before committing ourselves to a love relationship. I am convinced that if we become good friends with the potential mate before becoming a couple, that our chances of an enduring relationship are increased. It is during friendship where compatibility is discovered.

It is my opinion that human beings were not created to be owned by one another but to co-exist in harmony and in liberation. This is to say that any relationship, which imposes emotional or physical bondage on a person, is not giving value to individual wholeness. In a relationship we do not own the other person *individuality*. People must be given room to possess their values, uniqueness, and their friends without infringements upon those rights. Liberation is an expression of the presence of God's spirit. True love for a mate will allow us to release that person to have their friends. But each person in the relationship must know themselves as to whether they can handle having separate friends in a relationship. The relative question to ask is:

1. Will having separate friends be comfortable for me—and do my acceptances of it naturally and comfortably flow from my personality?
2. Can I be content with my mate spending time with an old friend who might have been an ex?

If you cannot answer "yes," this would be a good place to start communicating your expectations and establishing boundaries for old friendships.

Article 26

Maintaining Your Identity
(Don't Loose Yourself in Relationships)

As individuals we take a lot of pride in our identity of *self* and in the accomplishments that we have made throughout our lives. Our self esteem and ego is consumed by how we are viewed by others and how much we are respected by the people we love. Even our occupations help us to identify, or at least gives us a perspective about who we are. Our self esteem is heightened when we feel admired by our friends and family and knowing that our lives means something to someone else. We relish in our identity. But what happens when we loose our individuality and identity in relationships? How do we loose it? How do we get it back? These are the questions that I'll be addressing throughout this article.

People have the tendency to give more of themselves in relationships than what they're *consciously* willing to give. After giving so much of their love, affection, resources, time and attention, they unfortunately feel a sense of regret afterwards if it goes unreciprocated. When a person gives of themselves in a relationship and it is unreciprocated, they will begin to feel devalued. An aspect of our human need is to feel valued and accepted and when what we give is perceived as not being appreciated or accepted, we feel rejection. When we feel rejected as a person, we will begin to loose our personal identity in the relationship—feeling that we are not enough or that we are not appreciated by the person we love. As I stated in the beginning, that part of our identity is connected to how we are perceived by the people we love. Often women are the victims of this dichotomy, because of the nurturing character that women innately possess—their need to be a *giver* to their loved ones. And if the woman's giving is not equally matched, or as she *perceive* equal—she will regret giving so much when her giving is not valued. People also feel that they are unappreciated when they give of themselves, and their efforts of trying to please go unrecognized. This can often be interpreted as the *receiver* being ungrateful—especially if the *giver* fails to understand that people reciprocate differently.

To answer the first question, this is how we loose our identity—when we give too much of ourselves. We begin to loose our personal identity when we unrealistically think that people are going to give to us in the same manner that we give to them. We all have different value systems, meaning that we hold some things in higher esteem than others—depending on our frame of references or experiences. An example of having different value systems is when a man shows his love for a woman by being the best provider he can be, which might entail working long hours to provide her with the things she want. On the other hand a woman might show her love to a man by showing him affection, cooking a special meal or maybe something as simple as running errands for him. Both individuals are expressing their love for one another however different if may be, and though the actions are different, yet the expression of their love for one another is equally genuine.

In answering the second question, this how we get our identity back. Never *give away* more of ourselves than we are willing because we are truly "giving away" a part of ourselves when expressing our love. This simply means that however we give—do it without the expectations of a return. This will prevent us from experiencing that sense of "loosing ourselves" to another, or loosing our personal identity. We maintain the constancy of who we are as an individual when we stay connected to our own needs and desires—not giving away that part of ourselves in which we desire to keep.

To regain personal identity, we must also recognize our uniqueness, and our value as an individual—because there is not another like us in the whole universe. This self awareness is crucial because if we fail to possess this healthy sense of *self*—our self value or self esteem will diminish—resulting in a feeling of unworthiness. It is a direct violation of our personal *will* when we allow ourselves to give beyond our comfort. We should never feel imposed upon to give what we cannot afford to give whether emotionally, financial, or simply our time. We must take back our power of self ownership and become selfish, meaning having a sense of ones' self or needs, as I related in article 12 **Why Should I Be Selfish**.

We must consciously restrain ourselves from giving to the point of feeling emotionally bankrupted. Do not give to receive—for this will keep us in control of our emotions. Finally, do not connect your identity to things that do not define your character. Your job and your cars, houses and financial status, or even associations to name a few, will never define the true essence of your *being*. Materialistic things will never define the glorious *spirit* that you are. People place too much interest in physical things—and in the opinions of others. We as individuals are far more than other peoples' expectations and our value surpasses any measure of anything materialistic.

If we can free ourselves from the outside influences and drown out the noise of the worlds' opinions of what we as an individual should be, then we can maintain the identity of our true and healthy *self*.

Article 27

Compatibility & Love

I am very passionate about this subject so I will be speaking very in-depth on this matter. At times it may seem that I am straying from the central point but continue to read and you will clearly see the connection.

Which is most important in a monogenic love relationship—compatibility or love? As I reflect back to the demise of my past love relationships, I concluded that most of them ended because of incompatibility. Every failed relationship that I have had as an adult, has been with women who were of quality and class but the problem was that we *did not* or *could not* find that medium or place of compromise in our expectations of one another. Our core values and core convictions did not line up so that we could fulfill one another's expectation in the relationship. No matter how much we loved each other, we just couldn't get alone—therefore we became frustrated with one another and grew apart. So I believe compatibility to be the most important factor in a long term relationship. When I would hold couple's discussion groups, I often saw that many of their issues also stemmed from incompatibility—in one area or another.

Compatibility is defined as being in harmony with, well matched, suitable, or to be congruous. I would like to add that compatibility is the *essence of mutuality*. I will refer back to each of these definitions, but first I need to explain what I mean by compatibility being the *essence of mutuality*. The *essence* is what makes anything what it is. For example—the essence of an apple is its seed—it is the core or root of what make anything what it is. The core or essence of compatibility is mutuality meaning having things in common—thereby developing this term *essence of mutuality*. Compatibility is the fundamental nature of having common interests or needs. All healthy relationships must have a common interest, common fundamental belief system, and mutual expectations in order for the relationship to grow. But there are other crucial dynamics to a healthy relationship which relates to the "wholeness" of the individuals coming into it.

The first question to ask ones' self is, "Am I compatible with myself ?" How many of us are truly harmonious or in congruency (in agreement) with *self*? How many of us truly love and respect *self*? Many people have failed relationships because they have failed to have a healthy relationship with themselves first. People often live self destructive lives which reflect their being out of harmony with themselves. An example of being out of harmony with ones' self includes activities such as illegal drug use, stealing, killing, cheating (in all regards), staying in abusive relationships, harboring bitterness (not forgiving), and any other thing that causes our conscience to feel conviction or guilt. But not everyone will have the same convictions about what is appropriate or inappropriate. Nevertheless, most people would feel that these are all bad behaviors—which includes any act that causes an individual to feel less than whole or guilty and cause them to be out of harmony with themselves. Any time a person do something to themselves that they feel guilty about already knows it's bad for them. In such cases self love and self worth is lacking. It is only until we harmonize and become in congruency or agreement with *self*, will we be able to harmonize and live in agreement with another.

We cannot continue to look unto others to make us whole or complete, because almost everyone else is looking for someone to complete them. It is like twenty children all trying to play with the same toy at one time—someone will be disappointed. The same is happening in the world of relationships. We all want the one toy (the perfect person) that nobody truly possesses. None of us at our best is perfect, because to someone else, you will be lacking something they need in a relationship that you will not be able to provide. When we are in pursuit for someone that's whole and complete—someone who has it all together—how can we realistically expect to find the perfect person when we are not? How can we bring our bitterness to someone else's bitterness, our baggage from previous relationship to someone else's baggage from their previously bad relationship, our hurt and distrust to someone else's hurt and distrust, and expect to have a harmonious relationship? The only realistic thing to expect in such a case is another disappointing relationship. And because we are creatures who need love and companionship—we continue to search for someone to share our lives with in spite of our imbalances and lack of wholeness. We must find our wholeness so that we are bringing workable qualities into a new and wholesome relationship.

People often continue hoping for the perfect person to come along, even when they have not addressed the issues of *self.* We find what we believe to be love—it often turns out to be mere infatuation. Until we discover the God within us—the wholeness we truly are, we will never experience a fulfilling love relationship. It is impossible to love ourselves completely until we understand who we are—and that our essence is God. To further elaborate on loving one's self—when we fall in love with ourselves, we are falling in love with the creation that we are—for we are the expression of God in human form as I've stated throughout this book. So when we mistaken love for infatuation because we're unable to properly discern, we find ourselves emotionally dependent upon another to fulfill within us what we cannot fulfill for ourselves. Too often what people relate to as love sometimes turns out to be nothing more than codependency (the need to feel whole or complete based on someone else's acceptance of you.) The pseudo or false wholeness that is felt by the codependent person is short-lived when the partner becomes absent of the relationship. A person then looses that *feeling* of wholeness, because in reality the person had not yet discovered their true wholeness. It is not enough to simply *feel* like you're whole just because of external circumstances that make you *feel* good—you have to be whole from within. Wholeness is a progressive work that manifests through periods of our lives—that is actuated through life experiences which brings about growth. No one can "grow us up"—only life and its experiences can do that. So we become whole incrementally in various aspects of our *being*.

Considering the dynamics referring to one's wholeness and harmony with *self*, which I believe to be the foundation for social harmony, compels me to believe that compatibility is most important in a monogenic relationship, because it encompasses getting to know a person from the inside out. Compatibility is often missed because people tend to establish romance before establishing true friendship. They feel that just because they have *things in common* that they know enough about one another. But having common interests with a person does not necessarily equate to being compatible with them. Having things in common like enjoying the same foods or movies, liking the same colors, enjoying the same activities just to name a few does not equal longevity in a relationship. Of course, all of those things are good and it is great having someone who shares similar interests, but it does not equate to compatibility. Compatibility also involves a connection on a spiritual level (that I will address at the end of this article) and not just the superficial things I mentioned above. But within the friendship stage you come to understand your likes and dislikes about one another and it is during this time that you see whether there is compatibility. We experience freedom when we are not required to alter who we are just to be with someone. The sense of being one's self lends to the foundation of a good relationship. This is why I believe that the friendship stage is so important because it allows us to grow unrestricted or confined to the norms and expectations of a love relationship.

Compatibility stems from our core needs and convictions as I alluded to earlier. It houses the contents of who we are on a spiritual level, and reveals the essence of our belief system. It is sometimes rooted into our DNA, and influences our decisions in life, and our perception of the world. An example of what I mean by compatibility being rooted into our DNA is in the case where a child inherits the parents' likes and dislikes, or inherits the parents' inhibitions and fears. Core convictions or beliefs can be either taught or inherited to a child. In the case where a parent is deathly afraid of dogs and teach the child to also be afraid of dogs will transcend the message to the child that dogs are dangerous. This message can be taught to the child subliminally (through parents' behavior) or taught by spoken words. In either of these two cases, the child would be considered as pre-exposed to a belief system that the child has no control over. This belief system whether true or not would become a part of the child's personality. Now this same child who has now become an adult might very well be drawn to someone who shares that same belief that dogs are vicious—and in that regard the two would be compatible because they would both have a fear of dogs. On the other hand if a person who is afraid of dogs becomes enlighten about dogs and no longer fear the idea of being harmed by them— the old belief system diminishes. Now they could meet someone who is a dog lover and would be compatible to them because of their new belief about dogs. This is just an example of how compatibility works from different dynamics, but this could relate to any area or levels of differences. As it relates to relationships, there is an even deeper level that I am making reference too in this article about compatibility—a level that transcends into spiritual and religious beliefs. When belief systems are in harmony it becomes the ingredients for a strong foundation to a meaningful, lasting relationship. This is because we as human beings are more spiritual in nature than we are physical. When our needs are of a spiritual nature, compatibility is very important because our belief systems run deep into who we are.

It is good when we find someone who has the same spiritual/ religious qualities as our own. Sharing the same spiritual/ religious interests is a major component to a lasting relationship. This is because it is easier to fall in love with someone whom you share deep values with.

If you are seeking someone to grow old with, do not invest your time romantically with someone that you are certain to be incompatible with. There is always the possibility of falling in love. Falling in love with someone that you're incompatible with can be a huge trap for yourself—because it becomes hard to separate yourself once love sets in. I believe that it is easier to love someone you are compatible with than to "become" compatible with someone you love. Think about that statement for a moment! Falling in love is the most natural act of human beings. So let us not put so much effort in trying to find love—simply allow love to find you. And in the meantime, love yourself!

> *Love will always follow friendship and friendship will always harness love—for it is easier to love someone you are compatible with than to "become" compatible with someone you love.*

J. Meddling

Article 28

Perception Transference
(I am not "You")

There are some who feel that the world would be a better place if only the world would adopt their way of thinking. They don't actually say this of course but their actions and mannerism projects it. They feel that others should think and act the way they do. When I meet people like this, I now understand that there are elements of insecurities underlining their issue that lead them to this rationalization. We have all met people who proposed an opinion on something and try and subject everyone else to them. For example, they feel that if they lie and cheat—then the rest of the world must also lie and cheat too—or if they enjoy *Life Time* movies surely everyone else enjoy them as well. But the reality is that everyone is not the same—and I am not you and you are not me. All of us from time to time struggle with the differences that we have with other people—but we understand that our differences should not be superimposed upon them. Many potentially great relationships are destroyed in the beginning with this belief that we must see and understand things the same in order to have a good relationship. This belief that we have to be the same is what I relate to as **perception transference**—when one person attempts to transfer their beliefs, habits or lifestyle upon another, based upon their own perception.

I had a friend who became romantically interested in me, but because I never made advancements on her, she assumed I was gay. I did not understand why she felt that way about me, seeing that we only considered ourselves friends—so I felt no reason to cross that line with her. She had known me for several years and had always known me to be a "strait" man. But what I remembered about her was that she had experience being in a relationship with a woman years prior to meeting me. I remember her sharing with me about a relationship she was in with a woman and that she was only experimenting with her sexuality. However, she did not consider herself a lesbian just because she was going through an experimental stage with a woman. She stated to me how that she felt like she was an attractive woman and that any man uninterested in her would have to either be gay or trying to figure out his sexuality. Because of her past experience she felt that I was going through an experimental stage with men just as she went through with a woman. Now how messed up is that! I was so surprised that she was relating to me in such an obscured manner. Though she may not have been conscious of her perception, she evidently proposed that thought. Sometimes it's a matter of the other person wanting you to have the same *perceived* weaknesses as theirs in order to feel equal.

Since then, I have encountered **perception transference** on so many other occasions that I can easily identify it when it is present. Unconsciously, many people operate in this reality every day. They believe that if they struggle with something you too must struggle with it. This is why I believe that most people who have been "cheated on" or who have been the cheater find it difficult to trust a partners' faithfulness in the relationship. If you used to cheat in relationships, chances are you might be suspicious of others cheating on you in a relationship. This not only applies to cheating but to something as simple as keeping your promises. If you seldom keep your promises, you might have a hard time believing that others will keep their promises to you. This mentality can be portrayed in any area of our life where we are insecure with ourselves.

As I alluded to earlier, that "wrong" perception can destroy a potentially good and healthy relationship at the beginning—therefore we must try and see the good in others. We must teach ourselves to see the good or the God in people, and not subject who they are to our perception of who we are. We must see that people are potentially good regardless of their differences to our own. This however does not mean that we do not allow ourselves to discern or see the truth about people—but understanding that others do not have the same hang-ups or experiences that we have. People who live with a pure and honest heart see things purely and honestly. But people who live in guilt or shame or have regrets of their own lives will despise the lives of others.

I believe that human beings are created innately "good," but somewhere along the line of life, we have confused or simply never understood our individual God given goodness. We have not learned to perceive life through the eyes of God who abides within us. When we fail to see the good in ourselves, we are also failing to see the God who lives within us—and will struggle with identifying the good in rest of the world.

I am not you—and you are not me, but we are all part of this wonderful universe where we were meant to live by the support of one another through the power of Higher Intelligence. Let us live, laugh and enjoy the differences of one another—awaken to the awareness that we are all one—created equally but as individuals.

Article 29

Life after Disappointments

Like a boxer who is disoriented by a punch, "takes a knee" (to kneel on one knee as to take a time-out) to reestablish his senses—so must we when regaining our senses after facing disappointments. No matter how much we pray and believe, we will always have to deal with the jolts of life. It would be helpful if we see disappointments as a vehicle that brings *self* to a deeper awareness of the God of the Universe. People less frequently practice self evaluation when all is going well—just as the boxer sees no need to change his fighting strategy when he is winning. We should always give attention to our *inner self* because we will experience fewer disappointments in life when we concentrate on feeling "whole" within ourselves. The Universal God is always in communication with our *inner self* or spirit—but failing to take the time to quiet our spirit and centering ourselves causes us to miss the divine instructions that come from within.

Disappointment comes in every form imaginable, but some can be more devastating than others—especially in the case of a break-up in a relationship. One reason that break-ups in relationships are so painful is because much of our *self identity* is wrapped up into it. We are innately dependant upon one another for physical, emotional, and spiritual survival. Our need for one another is part of a survival mechanism placed into the threads of our humanity. People define who they are by the relationships they establish. We feel good about ourselves when we are surrounded by people who validate our worth. No matter how good our friends are to us, they cannot protect us from the disappointments of life. Just because we are knocked down in the first round of life, does not mean that the fight is over. How many times have we seen a boxer get knocked down in the early rounds of a fight? And then that same boxer recomposes himself to win the fight! Life is no different. It is simply a matter of understanding that in life there will be many challenges and battles to win. When we understand that we have been prepared from birth for this life that we have entered—we can then draw from that assurance that we can, and will recover from every challenge.

The key to overcoming disappointments is to not focus or give attention to where you are in the present, but focusing on your anticipated future. Do not focus on past mistakes and misfortunes. Instead, move your thoughts and attention forward to a place in your *inner self* that makes you feel whole and complete. It does not matter what the negative emotion is, whether its feeling bad, angry, hurt or rejected, they are all feelings of disappointment. Focus on the good that you wish to feel, and you will multiply the positive emotions that brings positive manifestations. You will become a testament to yourself that you can overcome every disappointment. More importantly, you are a co-creator with the God of the Universe, who work through, and with you to make your life what you choose it to be.

Article 30

The Rejection Games

How often have we seen or experienced rejection in a relationship—and how it hurts? We've even seen how people have fought to stay with a relationship when the other person has moved on with their lives. Those who have been rejected sometimes already known that the other person had been looking for a way out of the relationship for a long time—and yet the rejected person still try and hold on. Another scenario of the rejection game is when a person who is being pursued for a relationship—rejects the "pursuer." The moment the "pursuer" gives up on the pursuit, the one who rejected now becomes interested in the one that they earlier rejected. At some place in our lives we may have experienced someone who was interested in dating us that we were not interested in—but as soon as our pursuer move on to someone else, we decided that we were now interested in them after all. These are the issues of what I call the Rejection Games!

It is interesting how we as human beings try and hang on to people or things once we have forfeited them. It shines a light into our psyche of how greedy or protective we can become when giving up something or someone, we don't even want. I do not believe that we consciously play this game, but it is innate to our human characteristics. I learned from many years in sales that it is important to give the customer a sense of ownership to the product—by having them to touch the product, test drive it, taste or smell it, or to try it on for size—whatever it took to make the product feel like it was theirs. Creating the sense of ownership is what stimulates the human ego to possess. Once we test drive the car we like, we feel that there is no way we can leave that car on the lot for someone else to drive home. We are exactly the same in relationships—and in some very extreme cases there are those who aren't willing to release others from their lives—so they physically abuse or threaten with harm, and even murder to maintain a *sense* ownership. We are not objects to be owned or controlled, for we are born to be free individuals. Nevertheless, none of us enjoy loosing the people or things that we want.

This rejection game can have various scenarios to it. There are people who fear rejection so badly that if they sense that a boyfriend or girlfriend is anticipating on breaking-up with them—they will create disharmonies to distract negative focus from themselves so they can be the one to initiate the break-up first. This is the same scenario that is played when a boss tells the employee that "You're fired!" The employee then responds by saying "You can't fire me because I quit!" This is simply the ego of the conscious *self* saying that "I own my destiny, and no one but me declares my fate"! We are not immune to accepting NO, because being made in the image of Higher Intelligence, we are internally wired or *spiritually designed* to achieve, to divide and conquer and to master. Our drive for life is unsurpassable—so when we are forced to face rejection, we quickly, and yet unconsciously go into our protection-mode. We protect an aspect of our very core of our conscious *self*—the ego. This protection sometimes resembles the attitude of "I don't care" or "I can take you or leave you" mentality. It may even display as the happy-go-lucky attitude that "I'm really all right . . ." But the most common responses are the ones of hurt, sadness and anger.

Unfortunately rejection is a painful part of our humanity and we must always bear in mind that we are not responsible for being everything someone else wants. We must also understand that it is not our responsibility to control others by manipulation, fear, deception or force. Lastly, we must remember that we are the most powerful force to be reckoned with on the earth and that our destiny lies within our own hands and not in the opinion of others. So let's keep it moving!!!

Article 31

Understanding the Role of People in Your Life

How often do we attempt to place people where "we" want them in our lives? Of course there is nothing wrong with that if they are willing to be where you place them, but often this is not the case. Others may not share our sentiments on the closeness of a relationship. This does not mean that they do not care or have love for us, but that they have a different perception of the dynamics of the relationship. For example, your housekeeper who cleans for you three days a week may not want to be your best friend. Their only interest is being your housekeeper. So when you ask them to hang-out or go shopping with you and they decline—you must understand that the dynamics of their relationship with you is perceived differently. I have seen this example of misinterpreted relationships played out many times and unfortunately the one who feels rejected often ends up disappointed.

There may be people that we would like to connect with, and have a relationship with, but if we are to have healthy and meaningful relationships—we should not try and force the relationship to happen. Attempting to restrict others into our world will only bring restriction to ourselves. When we attempt to control another person's behavior in a relationship, we stunt the friendship and loose our sense of *wholeness*. The God of the Universe never forcefully steer us into any direction—and neither should we to others. Of course there's nothing wrong with positioning yourself to meet someone to make a good impression on them, but let it rest with that. Allow God to connect the right people, at the right time, in the right place for you. All of the work involved in bringing the fulfillment of our lives is not in the work of our hands only, but understanding that the Universe is conspiring in our behalf. It is the work of the Universal God operating in us that gives us the confidence in knowing that we can sit back and allow the perfected course of things to take place in our lives. Outside of our conscious reasoning, God working through us knows the right person for us, and when to bring them into our lives. It is not necessary to try and orchestrate every detail of our life—for we in our carnal knowledge lack the ability to be accurate—but the Universal God within us knows all.

We should never try to force anyone into being a part of our life. When we attempt to force others into our lives, we are depriving them of their right of choice—just as we have the right to choose who we want a relationship with. We should never attempt to take a person's sense of empowerment by imposing our expectations of friendship upon them. Simply allow the relationships to be what they are. It may very well be that a person is meant to be an intricate part of our life at a latter time. Do not ruin it by attempting force. This is certainly true when it comes to a love relationship. In a potential love relationship—to push too hard can appear as desperate or needy—sometimes interpreted as weakness. Show the pride of your *inner self*, and be seen as the confident individual that you are, and watch the wonderful unfolding of healthy relationships manifest before your eyes.

Article 32

Questioning my friends?

I was having lunch in the terrace area of one of my favorite restaurant in Atlanta Georgia with some friends and colleagues when I heard my name screamed out from a very flamboyant voice. When I looked to see who it was, I noticed that it was a former student of mine name David, who is openly gay. I had grown to respect David—knowing his struggles and seeing how he rose to success. I was glad to see him, so I went over to greet him with the same enthusiasm as he greeted me. I introduced him to my "heterosexual" friends/ colleagues who were now standing at the table with there mouths gaped open with amazement of my acknowledgement of this obviously gay man. I offer my former student a seat at the table with me and my associates but he declined stating that he had errands to run. He thanked me for the offer and with all of the flamboyancy he could mustard up embraced me and said his goodbyes. My heterosexual friends were now relieved that this embarrassing gay man refused the offer to sit and eat with us. They once again stared at me for an explanation in which I felt no need to give them one. But, because of the awkwardness of the silence and the opportunity to show who my true friends were, I decided to explain the kindness I showed to my former student David. I began by saying: I know you are wondering—what does a heterosexual man like yourself have to do with a flamboyant homosexual? The thought was etched into their faces, so I proceeded to tell them David's story.

David is thirty two and contracted the HIV virus four years ago from his now deceased partner who died of AIDS. It was during this time I met him as a potential student inquiring about my class. Because of the turmoil in his life with loosing his lover and contracting the HIV virus, he decided to go back to school to rediscover a purpose in life—so he took my anatomy & physiology class. David was an excellent student with a 3.9 GPA, but he suffered from depression due to the recent loss of his lover. Five months into the course David began to miss days until he was no longer attending school. Because attrition was such a major focus at this school, the responsibility of attendance rested upon the shoulders of the instructors. So as an instructor, I decided to go to David's house to check on him since I could no longer reach him by phone. When I arrived at David's house and knocked on the door, I noticed that the door was already ajar so I went in and called for him. I knew something was terribly wrong. I went through his house screaming, "David where are you?" When I found him, he was in the fetal position in the bathtub half filled with water whimpering, wearing pajama bottoms. He stated to me that he had taken a half of bottle of sleeping pills along with some alcohol. He said that he had attempted to end his life and was about to fulfill his demise by cutting his jugular vein. That's when I notice the knife underneath his shoulder. Being lost for the right words at this crucial moment, all I could say was "No You Aren't!" You have a report due in three days and you are not going to mess up my class attrition by missing anymore days!" David looked at me shocked as to say, "All you can think of is your attrition?" He began to sob loudly and then a sequence of hysterical laughs and more sobbing. I cradled him and held him like an infant for about twenty minutes. David came back to school two days later with his report in his hand with a new zest for life. He still has bouts with depression alone with emotional issues, but more than anything David has a propelling desire for not being denied happiness. He later told me that the day I came to his house and saved his life, was the day that I saved the life of those who looked to him for strength. After hearing David's words, all I could do was shed the tears that had begun to fall. David added, "I have so many friends and clients who depended on me to keep them encouraged that the pressure had begun to weigh me down. Mr. J. (what my students called me) I could no longer bare their problems compound with my own. Thank you Mr. J. for going outside of your duties as an instructor and being a friend." I went on to explain to my associates at the table whose faces now quieted with embarrassment that David is a quite positive and influential businessman that many rely upon. It was in that moment that I realized the influence my life had on so many others through David's life. David in returned had given me life. This experience transformed my life by restoring my sense of purpose. It has become one of my motivations for writing on the subjects of finding wholeness through spirituality.

Peering into the eyes of each one my associates at the table I said to them, I know some of your darkest secrets as well as I know David's secretes. Just as I have befriended David a flamboyant homosexual, I have befriended all of you at your lowest periods in life. Even at this table of Christian heterosexual men and women, I have engaged in friendship—an abusive spouse, sex offender, one who cheats on income taxes, unfaithful in their marriage, lies about their income, and one who doesn't pay their debts—just to mention a few of your secrets. All faces at the table soften with shame. I continued by saying that David may be an embarrassment to you because of what he displays on the outward, but he is transparent to the world. You all on the other hand are impressive on the outward but have little integrity. You must bare the guilt of who you are on the inside—lacking real character. So if you care to question my friends, please start by questioning why I am associated with you!

> *If you determine a friend by the world's acceptance of them, then you have just determined that you are not a friend. It takes a person of confidence to stand with the unpopular.*
>
> J. Meddling

Article 33

When Sex Hurts

When we think of sex hurting, we might automatically associate the hurting to the woman—but in this article we will be addressing factors of hurt relating to sex from two categories. These categories are physical and emotional. With the consideration of these two categories, we can already see how this could affect both men and women.

Sex should not *merely* be about two people trying to reach an orgasm or "get theirs"—at least not in a love relationship. The greatest gift that a man and woman could give one another in the relationship is the **"gift of consideration"** (in which I spoke of earlier in article 13.) Consideration is when we look within ourselves and see the good that we desire for ourselves and lend it to another. The same concept should be applied to the bedroom if we are to experience the bliss of a true and meaningful sexual relationship.

If unnatural physical pain is apparent during intercourse for either partner, modifications in the activity need to be made. Maybe a change of position, less aggressiveness or whatever is needed to accommodate the other should be done. If the mans' aggression is the cause for discomfort ease up and practice a little tenderness. Secure and sensitive men do not need to prove their manhood by being rough with their women—especially if it's causing her discomfort. Sometimes men, who are overly aggressive in bed to the degree of causing physical pain without any care or sensitivity to their mate, might be displaying behavior reflecting insecurity or some type of physical or emotional abuse from their own life. It could be a case where they just do not care which poses an even greater problem within them. Nevertheless, aggression is often a manifestation of inward hurt or a need to control. In either case the man who possesses this behavior has not matured in true self love. True love for *self* will never allow one to consciously or maliciously hurt, harm or control another. True and mature love which reflects the nature of God, never disregards the needs of others. God never disregard or control human beings, but has allowed us to be creators of our own destinies.

On the other hand there are some aggressive women who inflict physical pain onto their men as a part of the sexual activity. These women are referred to as practitioners of dominatrix. A dominatrix (plural dominatrices or dominatrixes) is a woman who plays the dominating role in a sexual relationship. Another term used for this kind of bedroom control is sadomasochism commonly known as (S&M). Sadomasochism is the combined term referring to any persons who like to receive or inflict pain during sexual intercourse. Sadism used as a sexual term describes a person who takes pleasure in "inflicting" some form of pain on a person. Masochism describes someone who takes pleasure in "receiving" humiliation or pain from another. Men who are conservative in the bedroom may not particularly care for this type of bedroom energy, and might find it a little demeaning to their egos. However, a man's ego will often allow him to experiment outside of his comfort zone in the bedroom—especially if he is making the effort to allow his woman to be a little more creative in order to please her. Nevertheless, pleasing a sexually demanding woman who enjoys inflicting pain should never cost a man his dignity, even if he is seeking to please his woman. Women need to be sensitive too!

The other element of experiencing hurt during sex relates to the emotional. Emotional hurt can come by way of insults about one's body, comparisons to previous lovers, criticizing one's performance, to name a few. All of these insults should be kept from the bedroom if a couple is focused on creating a bond and enhancing creativity in their sex life. There is nothing worse to a man than to have his anatomy made fun of—or to feel disrespected and unappreciated. There is nothing worse to a woman during a time of intimacy in the bedroom than to be made to feel unattractive or undesirable by her man. Every woman wants to feel protected and cared for by her lover. Women thrive on being valuable to their partner and must be complimented often. Both men and women alike need to know that they can be their true selves in lovemaking without the risk of mockery, judgment, or discrimination. Sex should therefore, never hurt physically or emotionally or cause one partner to feel violated, shame, remorseful, disrespected or devalued. The acts of lovemaking is one of the most bonding gifts given to humanity—so let us entreat it with honor.

Article 34

Masturbation & Sex

One of the most avoided issues talked about especially in religious circles is the topic of masturbation. Yet, masturbation is one of the most primitive and privately practice activity among people of all races, creed, color and even religion. It is interesting to me how that some people (usually religious people) view masturbation as being the "great dark evil," and yet I am discovering through statistics and surveys that I've done—that they are the biggest practitioners of the act.

Masturbation defined is: self excitement or stimulation of the genital. It is also called *onanism* by many religious sectors—meaning self abuse. In the biblical texts where it is named after "Onan," a man mentioned in the Old Testament in Genesis 38: 9 who ejaculated onto the ground and who was considered committing a sin. Onan broke the law of tradition by not impregnating his deceased brother's wife, which was the custom of that day to insure that the family name of the deceased brother would be carried on by the sons of Onans' seed. You would have to read the whole story to understand the customs of that time and the reason why it was considered a sin. Nevertheless, masturbation is a reality in most cultures, and is not an act of sin or viewed as self abuse by most customs. The denotation that masturbation is self abuse, therefore making it a sin—is restricted to a few religious interpretations. Webster New World Dictionary simply defines *onanism* as the withdrawal in coition (vaginal penetration) before ejaculation. Webster Dictionary does not define it as an act of sin.

In gathering information for this book, I have talked and surveyed many people on the subject of masturbation and asked—why do "you" do it? The answers have been pretty much the same for men and women—and that would be the most obvious—it's pleasurable! But I have heard a few responses that caught my attention. One woman stated to me that when she masturbates she feel loved by herself. I then asked her to explain and she said "when I masturbate, I feel a connection with myself just as I would feel a connection with a lover. I feel a sense of respect and self appreciation in knowing that I do not have to sleep around to experience sexual fulfillment—I am self contained." She continued by saying that masturbation was emotionally and physically safer for her because she did not have to struggle with the possibility of being told by a lover that they no longer wanted to be with her. Women in general stated that masturbation freed them from the worry of getting STDs or pregnancy. Other women added that orgasms from masturbation were more intense than it was with their lover. These statements engaged me into a processing of theories and ideals as to why some people (particularly women) feel more enjoyment in the act of masturbation than sexual intercourse. When I asked a group of men about masturbation, a good 97% of them felt that it was a natural act for a man. Most of these men said that they find it to be an enjoyable act right after having sex with their mates—and that it was the norm!

Men and women have expressed that after having their first or second child, that masturbating was their favorite pass-time. This probably lends to the busy schedules that comes with having a family. The energy levels of both partners in a family setting typically are much lower than that of single individuals who have no children. Often one partner feels abandoned when the children come along—typically it is the man. However, some women have expressed that they have experienced feelings of neglect by their men when a child came into the picture. I believe in these cases that the men were incorporating more working hours to support their growing families, while the wives was lacking and craving the sexual attention they once got from their mates before children came along. Having children in the house can cripple couple's intimacy faster than anything—especially if it's combined with feelings of not being the center of their mate's attention. This is true for men and women. Regardless of gender, we all have the same basic needs in a relationship—the need for love, respect, assurance, devotion and pleasure are basic human needs. A small group of my interviewees and surveyors said that masturbation was as much of importance to themselves, as being loved by their mates.

As part of the sex conversation in a group discussion—I asked a group of men out of curiosity about being vocal in the bed room—and I got some very interesting responses. To my amusement, some men felt a little apprehensive about being verbally expressive during love making. They shared confidentially that they felt somewhat embarrassed if they were too verbally—feeling like they had to maintain a level of control as a man. Other men expressed that they would feel like a "punk" if they screamed or shouted louder than the woman during lovemaking. One guy said that a woman might loose a level of respect for his manhood if he was to start expressing himself like "some little girl." Another guy told me that it was outright feminine to make any sounds outside of a grunt during lovemaking. Considering myself as an evolved "brother," I felt that these guys had massive insecurities.

On the other hand, when asking women about how they felt about verbal expression during lovemaking, most of them had no problem with expressions of any sort. There were a few religious women who expressed that women should not be vocal during sex, because the enjoyment of sex was primarily for their husband. *Probably not a lovemaking session that most men would want to be a part of!* Out of curiosity I asked these same religious women who did not believe in being verbally expressive in lovemaking about their perspective on masturbation—and many of these women expressed to me (in their own way) that they believed that masturbation was evil. I hate to say it, but having observed human behavior and observing body language during counseling sessions for so many years, I knew they were not telling the truth—in fact, I believe that masturbation was their best friend.

For many, masturbation provides a connection with one's self and relieves emotional and physical stress. However, if masturbation causes a person to feel guilt or condemnation, it might be wise for the sake of their conscience or *inner self* not to do the act. Getting an understanding of the "guilt" associated with this act needs to be evaluated. Sometimes people carry unmerited convictions that have been passed down from generations. Religious belief systems often rob humanity of righteous pleasures and activities.

Article **35**

Understanding *"Self"* in Sexuality

(View on Men)

Sexuality is defined as: Capacity for sexual feelings or the quality of being sexual. I would like to add for the sake of this article that sexuality is one's view or perception of how they see or feel about themselves sexually. Men sexuality just like women stem from the *essence of self.* We often relate to the males' *sense of self* as egoism, but it is no different than being in awareness of one's own needs and desires as I mentioned in article 12 **Why Should I Be Selfish**. Though we are taught that to be self centered and egotistic is a negative thing, it is however the awareness of self in operation. Nevertheless, the unhealthy view that a man might have about himself can sometimes cause struggles in his sexuality. Men unlike women are usually more aggressive when it comes to expressing sexual needs and desires. Though men are typically the pursuer, some men have identity crisis with *self* that inhibits them from projecting confidence when it comes to approaching women sexually.

Some of these inhibitions are generated from sexual, physical, or verbal abuses that they may have suffered from their youth. If a man has been abused in any one of these areas as a child, his lack of self confidence might manifest in a relationship as brutishness—the need to have dominance as an adult that he did not have as a child to protect himself. He may also lack sensitivity towards a woman in intimacy—for the nurture that he was neglected as a child that he fails to show in adulthood towards his mate (covered in article 33 **When Sex Hurts**). If he has experienced verbal abuse as a child this usually manifest in his adult life as being verbally abusive to others. Because of his inability to express himself without anger or profanities, he will lack the ability to effectively communicate his feelings to his woman when he is feeling inadequate. This is why I believe some men call women "bitches" and "ho's" and many other derogative names during arguments—lacking the skills to communicate effectively the hurt or disappointment that's being felt at that moment. This of course is not applicable to all abused men, but to the ones that's challenged with self identity issues. Verbal abuse on a child often leaves more permanent scars emotionally than physical abuses. What I see when humans are broken or damaged in their psyche is a profound need to feel *whole*, complete, and accepted. Whether male or female, we all have the same basic need—the need to feel accepted.

Men, just like women need to feel attractive and appreciated in order to be balanced in their sexuality. A man flirting is a healthy sign that the man is in a good emotional *place*, and possess a healthy image of himself. However, this harmless flirting should not be in the presence of his woman if he intends to have a harmonious relationship. I just felt the need to say that! I have also observed a positive change in a man's self image after becoming a father. It is a real boost to a man's ego when he has played a part in a life coming into the world—even if the man fails his responsibility to "father" the child. For some men, making a baby gives them a sense of manhood which makes him feel potent and sexy. Yes, men feel sexy too—just like women! And like women, men should make time for themselves by doing things they really enjoy. This form of showing self appreciation adds to his healthy emotional state. It is not about him being macho or egotistic—but about honoring himself and giving attention to his own needs.

Again, male and female alike have the same basic emotional needs. We need to feel validated, appreciated, love and respected. When these emotional needs are fulfilled—we feel good about ourselves and our sexuality or our quality of being sexual is heightened. This kind of healthy attention feeds our sense of sexuality. As we embrace our sexuality as men—let us be mindful to think well of ourselves and to live in the bliss and sexual excitement we were created in.

Article 36

Understanding
"Self" in Sexuality
(View on Women)

It is from a woman's *sense of self* that her sexuality or interest in sex is formed. Sexuality is the quality or state of being sexual. In my words: sexuality is one's view or perception of how they see or feel about themselves sexually. Many women (at least in my observation) are challenged in matters of their sexuality. I am not speaking of challenges in the sense of sexual orientation in regards to being lesbian. But I am speaking of the challenges that women have in seeing themselves as sexy—those who lack sexual confidence because of their obscured *sense of self*. I have found that the lack of sexual confidence is quite prevalent with women in our Western culture than any other place I have traveled. In my observation, Western cultured women are very sexually inhibited in comparison to other countries. Now I am certain that this is not inclusive to all Western cultured women, but I've observed that women in the European countries are much more liberal and expressive about their sexual needs and preferences than Western women. I have also observed more sexual liberties in other parts of the world in comparison. So I admonish women to possess and maintain a healthy perception of their sexuality by doing things for yourself that makes you feel beautiful and loved. Spending a day at the spa or the hair salon or something less expensive as getting a manicure and pedicure may be all that's needed to change your perception of *self*.

Women who have a poor sexual image of themselves will experience unhealthy sexual relationships. Sometimes these poor sexual images that women possess are rooted in sexual abuse, physical abuse or emotional/ verbal abuse.

Because women are typically more emotionally based, verbal communication plays a huge role in a woman's psyche when it comes to her feeling sexual. In order for her to have a healthy sexual relationship, she must be free to communicate any insecurity she might have about sex. A woman's security is the doorway to her being able to feel good about who she is as a sexual being. Therefore, an open dialogue about her and her mate's fears, taboos, and expectations is the foundation for a healthy sexual relationship. For the women who are not sexually liberated, an understanding of sexuality is essential before there can be ecstasy in lovemaking. For many women, the ecstasy does not happen automatically when they have insecurities. If a woman is to experience sexual fulfillment from her mate on an emotional/ spiritual level, she must first be self validated. She must possess that sense of sexual confidence that also stems from being admired and appreciated by her mate. And as well as being validated by her partner—she must validate herself. It takes practice and self observation to master the sexual fluidity and confidence that comes with being sexy.

Women who are shy or inexpressive in the bedroom are often dealing with identity issues about their sexuality. Once again, this is not an all inclusive statement because some women just aren't verbally expressive in bed. However, in my personal observation of surveys that I took—African American women had more sexual inhibitions than any other group of women in the Western culture. These same African American women also confessed to me their innermost insecurity relating to sex in a discussion group where only women, but of various races participated. I personally believe that these issues take their roots all the way back to slavery when Africans was stripped of their identity, culture, beliefs and pride. African women were separated from their husbands and children and were made to be the white owners sexual slaves alone with many other degrading duties. These women were simply raped physically and emotionally—loosing all sense of value. I believe that this played deeply into the psyche of black women inheriting their African ancestors' sense of degradation. This kind of subjection in my opinion distorted black women's identity of self and has been passed down for generations. (Read this book as a reference to sexual history and women in slavery: Horny & Saved by Sandra L. Snowden pages 16-17 Historical Evolution of Sex). Another factor for the loss of sexual identity among black women (and women in general) may be related to what is taught in churches and synagogues. The teachings of submission and subjection and the result of influences about sex that are hereditary may be partly responsible for the sexual insecurities that many women in our culture have. But women of every background and of every ethnicity struggle at some point in their relationships with the issues of their sexuality.

In some countries, social conditioning dictates that sexual pleasure is only for the man, and that women are only to be the providers of pleasure and children, and not the recipient. Even where this ideology is not verbally taught, it is however culturally expected. This mindset gives some understanding as to why these musical videos show multiple women half naked dancing seductively around one man—or men slapping women on their behinds with a dog chain around the women necks. The perception of women being in servitude to men is alive and well in many cultures—though servitude can be displayed in many other ways other than the one I've mentioned. This perception of women being subservient to men is fed subliminally into the mind of our society by way of media every day.

Women who have not awakened to their *feminine divinity* have adopted the mentality of worthlessness. Their *sense of self* is distorted by how the culture views them, and treats them as invaluable objects. No wonder women are loosing their sense of sexiness towards guys while some have turned to other women sexually because of feeling devalued by men. A woman will not have a good sense of her sexuality when she is unable to see her value.

This is why it is important for a woman to give value to herself. She should make the time to pampered herself—not waiting for someone else to show her the love that she already has for herself. This self romance allows her to grow more in love with herself—becoming more confident in her expressions and sexuality. Self romancing is simply doing those things for yourself that makes you as a woman feel sexy, loved and respected. To add to the suggestions I made earlier about women doing such things as occasionally sending roses to herself, buying herself sexy lingerie, treating herself to a fine dinning restaurant or planning a picnic with herself. These simple activities give a huge boost to the self image and lends to self love. Showing this kind of attention to yourself will help to validate your love for *self*, and will strengthen your sense of sexuality.

Article 37

Breaking Influences

Some of the hardest influences to break are those imposed upon us as children. These same influences or habits can become the most dominant controlling factors in our adult lives. An "influence" can be understood as any thing, person, or situation that sway or causes us to lean towards an opinion, creating our belief system. Sometimes people sway unwillingly to love one's belief system in order to get alone with them and to maintain peace in the household if they are living together. Often the need to maintain commonality (the need to fit in) is another reason people settle into other's beliefs. No matter the reason we are all influenced at some time or another into idealism or belief systems that does not match our core convictions. Most of us believe the things we're taught growing up as being *truth*, but often those things do not connect with our *inner self*. Our *inner self* or the God aspect of our *being* knows all truth and will not agree with that which is not true. This is the reason why some become dissuaded into belief systems that were not taught to them as children. Often people will having conflicting feeling about the things they grew up believing—but being unable to disprove those things because of the lack of enlightenment—many suffered with a conflicting belief system. The conflict was there all alone while they were maturing because the *inner self* was holding a truth that could not yet be understood or recognized.

Having the right influences in our life is vital because it is through our being influenced that we learn and understand behavior appropriateness, and to separate truths from facts. However, it is necessary to break the influences that take us outside of our core convictions. Any influence that prevents us from adhering to our own personal convictions should be shunned—even if we are unable to rationalize or make sense of those inner convictions. Remember, our *inner self* contains all truth. And if our core convictions are indeed mingled with misguided information through years of wrong teachings and bad influences—if we truly desire to become enlightened—the *inner self* will rise from within us bringing us the enlightenment that's needed. We can grow up believing that what we were taught as being truth turns out that in reality not to be. Nevertheless, we must live by our own constitution of right and wrong as long as it does not harm another. We can only live by the enlightenment that we have during that time.

Perhaps, if we are totally off-based in our belief system, I believe it becomes the job of the Universe/God to teach us through life experiences what is truth. No one has the infinite wisdom to teach or lead us on the path that is meant for our lives except for the Universe. If another tries to teach or lead us contrary to our own convictions, we will usually end up emotionally marred if we surrender to their belief. When people become marred by bad influences or teachings and loose sight of their own core convictions, the bad influences has to be broken in order for them to become whole. When our perception of *self* becomes devalued by bad influences, wrong decisions for our life always follow. An example of this is when the child who has been told repeatedly that they will never amount to anything, fulfill that belief by living a life of destruction. Bad influences can devastate lives!

Negative influences are not easily broken, because they are often intertwined into the core of our convictions—which are often rooted into years of misguided beliefs. Therefore, we must do diligence in breaking these influences by changing our association. If the misguided beliefs are a result of what we've been told as a child, then new positive influences will have to take place. I stated in the beginning, that the hardest influences to break are those imposed upon us as children. I believe the best way to reprogram "old mind-sets" is by finding new associations. When you transition away from people of negative influence, do not bother trying to explain your reasons for transitioning away from them—for they will never understand your rationalization until they become enlightened on their own path to spirituality. Look for people who are living in the "consciousness" that you are seeking. Associate with those who see you in a way in which you want to be seen—those who perceive you to be a good person. Observe if they live by their own convictions, and understand that they may not be the most popular in the mainstream circles. So prepare yourself to be among those who may not live by the orders of popular opinions. Seekers of truth usually run in smaller groups, especially those who have had bad religious experiences. These are the people (in my opinion) who are on the spiritual path looking for universal harmony and not possessing a hidden religious agenda. Seekers of truth are usually searching for their own way to wholeness and are not interested in converting others into their belief. Seekers of truth understand that every person has a built-in roadmap that can only be followed by the one who possesses it. They also understand that "truth" for someone else's life might be different from their own. Anyone who is trying to convert another to their belief system by stating that they have the "One Truth," avoid them! The Universe is multifaceted and carries many truths.

Secondly, to break negative influences—a change in our perception of who we are has to be re-introduced *to* and *through* our own mind. We must stop agreeing with the negative situations in our lives, and claiming them as our reality. Stop feeding into the negative belief systems that things must always be burdensome in life. If we are not making the money that we want to make, stop saying "I'm broke." If we are feeling lonely, stop confessing loneliness. If overweight, under weight, unemployed, fearful, sickly, or anything that creates negative feelings—stop proclaiming it as a part of your reality. Instead, start saying to *self* that my income is abundant, I am not lonely but surrounded by many friends, my weight is healthy, I am not fearful but courageous, I am not sickly but live in perfected health. In order for the outside situations to change, the inside perception must change first. Having a paradigm shift of *self* is essential for external transformation.

We cannot change other people lives by simply wanting them to change. Our responsibility to ourselves is to secure our own *wholeness* by breaking the negative influences that hinders our healthy perception of *self*. We are the beauty that we believe ourselves to be!

> *We change our lives when we change our association—we change the world when the world sees us changed.*

J. Meddling

Article 38

The Potency of Touch

Human beings can survive fairly normal without sight, smell, taste and hearing, but not without the ability to touch or feel. Out of our "five senses," touch scientifically is proven to be the most vital of them all. When we understand that there are approximately ten thousand nerve sensors in one square inch of skin, we can then appreciate the intricately designed sensory of touch. But this type of touch sensory is not the primary target of this subject matter that I am speaking of—but the ability to touch the human spirit with physical touch as well as touching with words and deeds. Nevertheless the same fact of the vitality of touch holds true. We cannot survive or maintain emotional balance without it because touch is the association to connecting with another person's spirit. In the late 1960s in a German hospital on the maternity ward where they kept a group of premature newborns, a female house-keeper would come by every night to pick up the trash from the nursery area. She had made a nightly habit of touching and holding the six premature infants that where closest to the doorway where all the trash was gathered. This was done over a period of three weeks. An observation was made that these six premature babies were out growing the other preemies in leaps and bounds. The doctors ran tests and checked their records for feeding schedules in trying to understand the reasoning of this obvious growth. The doctors could not find any variance in the care given to the six infants—until the house-keeper was later discovered giving the six infants the extra attention. So, the doctors concluded that it was without a doubt

125

because of the physical attention that these six babies were receiving from the house-keeper that they had outgrown the others.

Touch is powerful and crucial to human survival—for it is in the touch that an infusion of life and vitality is imparted from one to another. In ancient times before modern medicine as we know it, people would be physically and spiritually healed by the simple laying on of hands. Evil energies or demons as we relate to it in our modern day terminology were forced out of people by a touch from those who possessed supernatural good energies. Whether we believe in the healing gifts by the laying on of hands or not, the principle of touch causing a physiological change yet holds scientific truth. Being a teacher of anatomy, physiology and pathology—one thing that I know from a physiological aspect is that when you injure any part of your body and bring your hands to the injured area for comfort, that a super influx of blood rushing to the area (called hyperemia) bringing oxygen begins the healing process. Blood would naturally go to an injured area automatically, but it is proven that twenty percent more blood flows to the area when a "touch" aids the injury. I believe this to be the reason why we instinctively grab or hold an area when we feel pain in it.

There is another form of touch which is not physical that I mentioned in the beginning of this article. This form of touch is directed to the spirit of a person. Dr. Wayne Dyer stated in his audio book (Power of Intention) that one of the ways in which we declare the power found in non-physical touch is when we offer a public act of kindness. How we treat and interact with our fellow man promotes a physiological change in both our own bodies as well as the bodies of the observers. When an act of kindness is done publicly, serotonin is released into the nervous system causing a warm harmonious sensation in all who witnesses the act. Serotonin is a hormone that acts as a neurotransmitter providing a sensation of happiness and well-being. It is the "feel good drug" that our bodies naturally make when a good deed is done. Even the one committing the act of goodness is benefited.

I also believe that touch encompasses the affect that words have on our physiology. We use terms such as "I was touched by their story," or "she really touched my heart." This is proof that our body has stimuli to verbalization. Our inner *self* or spirit is in constant search for the right touch to validate our inner sense of empowerment. We need to hear periodically that we are doing a great job, or that we are appreciated, or that we are valued and loved. This type of validation gives a boost to the healthy aspect of the human ego as well as our physical being. These simple complements lay the groundwork for healing within a person on every level—the body, mind, and spirit which is the *inner self*. Have you ever been told that an outfit you were wearing was really nice—or that you were very pretty or handsome? How did that make you feel? Did you blush a little? It probably made you feel warm and appreciated causing you to blush. That blushing was the physiological change that took place in your body without anyone physically touching you. Blood rushed to the capillaries of your skin causing peach color pigmentation. This shows how much power our words possess and the changes it causes on a spiritual level. If we as human beings can have this much of a positive impact on one another, why don't we offer more of this healthy "touch" in a world starving for love and recognition?

Nothing can touch the human heart as deep as words—so choose your words with care.

J. Meddling

The Psychology of Dieting

There is such an insatiable need to loose weight and to look slim in our western society that new diet products are popping up everywhere and nearly every day. Dieting products and surgeries for weight reduction has become a multi million dollar industry. After spending hundreds and even thousands of dollars on weight loss, some people will unfortunately continue struggling with weight issues or eating disorders. This is because many do not understand the dynamic role that the psyche plays in dieting. The human mind, I believe, is the most powerful factor in loosing, gaining or maintaining weight. How we think can have a physiological affect on our metabolism.

Several years ago I taught anatomy, physiology and pathology as a part of a massage therapy course at Georgia Medical Institute. In addition to teaching massage modalities and ethics, I would encourage my students to eat and live healthy as therapists. I told them that the best diet to be on is the diet that allows you to eat "moderately" everything you wanted to eat. Focusing on what you cannot have only creates more desire for the food that you believe you shouldn't have—is what I stressed to them. Psychologically the perceived "bad foods" becomes a bad food for you. This does not only apply to food, but anything that has negative emotions connected to it—can become what you believe and causes a physiological change in the body. I continued by telling the students that if they would only incorporate a few simple exercises in their daily routine, (in which I incorporated thirty minutes each day in class) that they would begin to loose weight with only minimum efforts. I reminded the students of this fact every day for thirty days, and those who were interested in weight loss began to loose weight consistently.

In an article written by Holly Pinafore "How Your Thoughts Affects Your Metabolism"—Marc David, M.A., nutritionist and psychologist who founded the Psychology of Eating Institute in Colorado shares common thoughts on the subject. Marc David M.A. explains that 80% of digestion, relaxation, assimilation and calorie-burning power come from CPDR—cephalic phase digestive response. Cephalic means (of the head)—and studies showed that we needed to experience more than full bellies when trying to diet. We also need to experience taste, aroma, and satisfaction, in order to increase our digestion and calorie burning capacity. Marc continues by saying if I can paraphrase, that when we shovel our food down in a rush or guilty manner (believing a particular food to be bad), that we cannot properly digest or enjoy the taste of the food. When we stress over what is safe to eat, our bodies go into a defense mode causing hydrocortisone (cortisol) and insulin to release. This steroid hormone (cortisol) is secreted by the adrenal cortex and acts on carbohydrate metabolism and stores in the fatty tissues, causing weight gain. So we can see how our thoughts have a huge impact on our weight when we choose to fear food instead of enjoying it. This fear of food only increases the stress hormones cortisol and insulin.

So helping my students to simply change their mind-set about "bad foods," propelled them into healthier lifestyles and optimum health. And the stretching and flexing exercises that my students incorporated was so effortless that they would incorporate these simple techniques in their homes after school or work. Many of them to this very day continue to loose weight or maintain their size as a result of the exercises I taught them. One of my students in particularly was grossly overweight when she began my course and had what many of us would define as a poor diet. But this student continued with the new mind-set about food and continued her exercises two years after finishing my course. When I saw her two years later, I did not recognize her. It was only after starring into the students face that I remembered who she was. She carried herself with such confidence—something she did not possess two years earlier when she first came to my class. I remembered how she used to struggle with self esteem and weight issues—but not anymore! Needless to say, how excited I was to see a life so drastically, but wonderfully changed because of the knowledge that I had imparted about the psychology of dieting.

What we must understand is that when we think or believe a food to be an enemy to our health—we will manifest it into our reality. To further stress my point from a biblical perspective, this not only applies to food but anything that we have strong emotions or convictions about. In the Holy Bible; Romans 14:14 speaks to dietary issues and reads: . . . *but to him who thinks anything to be unclean, to him it is unclean.*

Discarding negative beliefs about foods would be a good place to start in the process of getting healthy. It would be a good idea to remove the word "diet" from our health vocabulary. The word "diet" currently carries a negative connotation or energy—loosing its true meaning which is "A Way of Life." The way we eat should become an everyday practice and not just a regiment to loose or gain weight. Another thing to consider for maintaining a healthy mindset about food is to eat your food in the present. When we eat in the present—we focus our attention on the flavor and presentation of the food—we observe the colors and aroma. We should anticipate the meal that we are about to enjoy, and savoring the experience of eating. Anticipating our meals before eating causes our mouth to salivate—creating saliva, which is the first neutralizing chemical process of breaking food down and preparing it for the stomach. Simply taking the time of chewing your food into a liquid state allows the mixing of chemicals in the saliva to aid in a healthy colon alone. There should always be a sense of gratitude for the provision. These simple suggestions will cause a healthy physiological change to take place in the body.

What I told my students years ago is what I believe today—eat everything you want in moderation—love your life and get plenty of exercise—and your body and life will always treat you well!

Article 40

Misinterpreting Human Behavior

Often we judged people's characters by their actions, and we ultimately categorize people as being bad or good. Behavior and deeds do not adequately reflect what is in the heart of the individual. How a person see themselves in their own minds, really defines who they are—even if their behavior contradicts the perception of how they view themselves. It is in our hearts or perception of ourselves that defines the truth of who we are. The Bible states: (paraphrased) "that human beings judge the outward appearance, but only God knows the heart of man." (1 Samuel 16:7). Religious people will counter that statement by quoting (Matthew 7:16) that read: "You shall know them by their fruits . . . ," insinuating that people are what they do—or that people are known by their actions or behavior. But people need time to mature into the masterpiece that they are innately—referring to living like the God within them. Many of the people that we wrongly judge or characterize as "bad" are still in the *seed* stage of their life. Most of us cannot identify a mustard seed from its full grown tree. Thus, many people are still in the seed stage of their life where behavior and intentions are often misinterpreted. Even when the "tree" is yet reaching maturity there can be confusion about what type of tree it is unless you know the seed that was planted and is a carpologist (one who studies seeds). The carpologist represents a mature discerning individual who understands that people need time to blossom and grow—one who understands spiritual development.

People go through many seasons in their lives and in the winter months, just like trees we cannot tell one tree from another when the leaves and fruit of that tree has fallen off. The same is true when people are in the winter transition of their lives. How many of us have drunk liquor and gotten drunk a few times in our lives? Does this constitute us as being an alcoholic? Have any of us ever experimented with drugs? If yes, does that qualify us as a drug addict? How many people out of curiosity have had a sexual encounter with someone of the same gender? Does that automatically make them homosexual? We could continue this list of questioning and the answers for most would be "No"! But not understanding what stage of life a person is in can lead us to judging them as a "bad" person when we see behaviors deemed inappropriate. The Apostle Paul states in Romans 7: 18—23 (paraphrased) "the good that I want to do, I don't do but rather I end up doing the opposite—the bad that I do not want to do, that's what I end up doing. Whenever I want to do good the evil that I do not want to do have a way of taking over. I have come to the conclusion that there is nothing inherently good in this flesh because it's always fighting against the real me who is a righteous and spiritual being."

The God nature or *seed of truth* within us is constantly manifesting its way into our conscious levels. But the growth may not look like what many might consider growth—it may appear as evil or bad behavior. How many of us have been caught in a bad situation where our reputation was marred—but later, that experience changed our life for good? This is the work of God's nature or *seed of truth* within us growing through our life experiences. We are becoming more like our Source, our essence, and our true self when we grow beyond our *perceived* bad experiences. A baby being birth into this world is not physically a pretty sight, but it takes that bloody and painful experience for that life to come into this world. It is absolutely no different in spiritual conception. God gives birth within us—and in time we mature into a whole *being*. God's seed is already in us which makes us innately good—but the growth that takes place in our lives may not always appear as "good" to others.

These statements are not meant to condone the irresponsible and careless lifestyles—but to encourage those who have been wounded by the judgments of others. I believe that the difference between people who are *purposefully* a menace to society and those who portray inappropriate behaviors is how they feel within themselves when doing bad things. If an individual enjoys being harmful or feared—it may be safe to assume that this is a true reflection of who that person is. On the other hand if a person feels remorseful of the bad that they do—it may be safe to assume because of their conviction of doing wrong—is a sign that this person is unconsciously reaching for their wholeness. What a person enjoys is the expression of their true nature. But if a person feels guilty about the acts they are committing—it is not reflective of that person's true character. The true essence of every individual is to be at peace and in direct harmony with the God within them. Therefore, if you are unhappy with yourself and are feeling conviction about any aspect of your life—you are not yet experiencing the wholeness of your true essence.

The man who finds peace within himself has found peace with God.

J. Meddling

Article 41

Loosing *Self* in Religious Addictions

In the seventeen years of serving as a counselor and life coaching people I have learned that people are conflicted with being able to portray to the world their "true self" for fear of offending the expectations of their religion. This conflict exists because religion by designed is meant to confine, restrict and constrain *perceived* inappropriate human behavior. But we all have our personal opinion of what we believe to be inappropriate. I believe that God never meant for humans to live restricted. I believe that many of the restrictions that religion has placed upon people are not exactly the order of God but of men to control the activities of its citizens. However, I do believe in societal order—but this order need only be enforced upon those who step out of its protection. Order is indeed protection for its citizens, but should never dictate a person's freedom to be or express who they are as long as their expression does not cause harm to others. Restricting a person from being who they are is a violation to our humanity. We are spiritual being learning how to exist in the confinement of human form. We innately resist anything that does not correspond with the identity of our essence which is *free spiritness*. I am not suggesting that there should not be structure and laws, binding to ordinances. However, when laws dictate the private activities of adult individuals—in which religion does—this is where I believe the conflict begins. I bear my own prejudice and biasness against what I personally consider as immoral activities, but I understand that the activities of others do not have to be a part of my experience. I simply believe that everyone has the right to chose what's appropriate and inappropriate for them, whether I or anyone else agrees. And if these inappropriate behaviors step outside of the guidelines of what the law of our land says, then consequences must be endured. For we are born into this existence with the understanding that rules and regulations are in place, so therefore we by our very existence in this era and form except these ordinances. But as citizens we can protect ourselves from the disappointment of our society by not giving attention to the things that's out of harmony with our preference. Our focus should be on the things that we desire in our realities, while allowing others the freedom to create there own experiences. We do not have to bash or be angry towards those who are not in agreement with our belief of appropriateness.

Religion is not a constitution of God, but is a man-made ordinance that is supposed to be established upon a divine truth or reality of God. Religion is also believed to be the expressed will of God for human beings lives as to what is appropriate and inappropriate behavior. We are taught that we are not free and that we are bound if we do not believe in God as a religion demands. Instead, religion gives dictations—serving as an angry taskmaster which only draws the negative emotions of those in opposition. This is why there are so many "holy wars" going on in the world—people attempting to control others based upon their religious beliefs. If everyone believes that their cause is the right one, and attempting to impose that belief on others, it will only keep the world in disharmony. If everyone understood their God given power (which embodies each one of us) there would be no need to rule, control, or constrain the practices of others. There would be no need to compete for sovereignty for we would only draw those who were in harmony with us—leaving the unharmonious out of our reality.

Religion demands attention to the ordinances given to rituals such as going to church, taking the Lord's Supper or Eucharist, fasting, and observing Holy Days, to name a few. There is nothing wrong with any of these observances in my opinion, but when one seeks to understand the *essence of the inner self* or the God within—the pure focus is sometimes lost by the combining of acts/good deeds to enlightenment.

In other words, people try and find God (who is already within them) by doing religious acts. But the essence of who we are (which is God) is being subdued by the very acts that are supposed to give awareness of who God is. We seek for God through acts and good deeds when God is within us all along. Even our personal aspirations get cloudy with religious dogma. For example: A person aspires to be a multi millionaire, but their religious teachings instructs them that all monies made beyond taking care of the basic needs have to be given charitably. This would be a direct conflict to what that individual wants for their life—living in the confines of what their religion is dictating. I heard in the Secret by Rhonda Byrne—"The Universe/God never tells you what you can or cannot have—the Universe only manifests in response to the request of the vibration stemming from your desires." So if a person believes that they are created for poverty or mediocrity, then the Universe will manifest that reality for them. Consider this true situation of a married woman with two children and an abusive alcoholic husband. She is affiliated with a religious group whose name I will not disclose. Her dream is to put her two children through college, but she needs to finish school herself to better her financial position. Her husband has not held down a job in two years, and is steadily putting her down for trying to do better. The woman wants to leave her husband thinking she would do better without him. But her church tells her that divorce is never an option and that if she proceeded with divorce that she would be excommunicated from the church. In a situation like this, how much liberty does this woman have in creating her own life when her emotional and spiritual support system fails her? So what I am seeing in this real life scenario is how religious practices can discourage a person from pursuing their God-given dreams. This is most definitely not the purpose of God indwelling us—so that we can be unproductive and unfulfilled?

Religion has become an addiction for many. Some people have become so caught up in doing good deeds for others that they often neglect the people that need them most—sometimes their own children, parents, or mates. After working in church ministries for more than thirty years, I have witness many pastor wives stray from their marriages, PKs (preachers kids) getting into drugs and all kinds of forbidden activities, becoming promiscuous—just to name a few. This by no means could be the work or the purpose of God—especially when family relationships are high priority with God (at least according to the Bible).

The act of neglecting the need of family or even yourself, for the sake of keeping religious practices is no different than that of a drug addict—who disregards the care of others so that he can get his "fix." All who are in close proximity of the drug addict will be affected negatively and will experience loss on some level. The same will be true for those who are religiously addicted—who disregard the cares of others to fulfill their religious dogma.

I am in no way bashing people who are religious, for I have my own personal rituals or religious acts that I do on a daily basis. My objective is to bring awareness to people who are denouncing their own personal joy and happiness to fit into a ritualistic community. We should never make an effort to fit into any group at the cost of loosing our individuality and happiness. We should seek associations with those who are in harmony with our personal belief system, and not those to whom we have to fit into their expectations.

Many people today do not ascribe to being religious but spiritual. To be spiritual simply means that they believe in God, Higher Intelligence, The Universe, or any other name identified as God, as a power or influence that is superior to us. It really has no relevance as to what name you call God. Spirituality is when a person seeks for truth (The Higher Power) from within his or her own *being* by sensing what's right and what's wrong and living thereby. What is important is that humans gravitate to the understanding that all that is needed in inheriting the life meant for them, resides in the intellect of the *inner self.* It is in the awareness of *self* that we rise to universal power—the power given to us by God. It is in the *self* that the mind of the Universe is being understood on a day-by-day journey. When we open ourselves to the Universe—not bogged down with traditions and ancient religious mindsets—that the unfolding of truth becomes alive within us.

Let's not seek a set of rules and regulations given thousands of years ago to control the behavior of a predominantly superstitious group of people. However, let us seek the fresh words of wisdom that flows from a universal, loving, all encompassing, non-judging energy. This energy is simply God, and it reflects the *essence* of who we are as human beings. We are God within ourselves, wrapped in human form, with multiple expressions, with faces of every color, tongues of every language, personalities of all sorts, and gifts and callings of all kinds. We are called to the higher level of *self*—as collective individuals joined together to create one universal love.

> *Where religion dictates, wars will fester.*
>
> J. Meddling

Article **42**

Heaven & Hell

(Literal or Mythical)

A question that I am frequently asked relating to religion is: "Is heaven & hell a literal place or is it simply imaginary?" I was cautious about answering because the people who usually ask this question typically did not possess the fundamental knowledge of the Bibles developmental history for me to even begin an intelligent dialogue. One must understand the basics as to how the Bible came into existence and its many developmental processes, before the authenticity of its words can be accepted as truth. Though I believe in the principals of the Bible, however I also believe that much of the interpretation has been manipulated through time by religious and political men to promote their own agendas. With that being said we must also understand that the translation of what's perceived as "truth" has not been completely represented in the writing of the Bible. And once again, I do believe strongly in the basic principles of the Bible—principles that support love, peace, and good will towards all people.

I believe that the original manuscripts (not completely added to our Bibles) was written to give hope and deliverance to a *perceived* fallen group of people, but once powerful and influential leaders saw how potent and powerful this written word was, and how they could control the people with it—a lust for power and dominance entered the religious arena. As a result of the powerful and influential needing to own and dominate the lives of people, the rewritten or partially written Bible was used as a tool or yoke of constraint. The Bible has been rewritten with major references left out—with the intention to control groups of people. It was used to manipulate the ignorant, the poor, the desperate and the superstitious.

Many slaves who were brought from Africa were persuaded to believe that in order to be a good Christian or follower of God—you had to be a faithful slave. The largest slave trade in the history of the world was created by Christian European nations. The **Atlantic slave trade** or **transatlantic slave trade** took place across the Atlantic Ocean from the 16th through to the 19th centuries. The vast majority of slaves transported to the New World were Africans from the central and western parts of the continent, sold by Africans to European slave traders who then transported them to North and South America. The numbers were so great that Africans who came by way of the slave trade became the most numerous Old-World immigrants in both North and South America before the late eighteenth century. Consequently, many slaves lost their inherent identity to a European belief system—a gospel that was not at all "Good News" to the slaves. Many of the slaves converted to a religion that gave no reference to their native spirituality, and showed no regard to their native history. They were then forced into the Europeans customs, traditions and belief systems even though the slave was considered no more than mere property. But forcing this new belief in hopes of slaves conforming to it made the slaves more manageable—because if you can change a person's belief about what's appropriate and inappropriate—you change their convictions which make them compliant. Therefore, as a tool of manipulation to guilt slaves into servitude, often the term "hell" was used by religious slave owners for a slave's disobedience. It was believed by the so–called good slave owners as being more humane rather than beating a healthy and hard working slave into submission. A healthy slave was more valuable to an owner than one that was beaten up and unable to work for several days. In the history of religion, brutish owners and leaders main objective was to isolate people from the knowledge of their heritage, to make them subjective or to exploit their skills. I am not a basher of religion and believe that there's nothing wrong with religion as long as it allow others to be free, and to practice their worship freely. But when religion enslaves or imprison by way of physical captivity, or emotional and psychological captivity—it is wrong.

What's crucial to understand is that religious leaders often have a political stake in society—and many unfortunately use their cloak of religion to control groups of people by fear and intimidation. Ignorant (unlearned) people were often made to feel that if they disregarded the laws set by the established Powers of that time—that they were also defying the laws of God. Without pointing a finger at any religious group, the early religious institutions and authorities, slaughtered many innocent people in the name of God—inferring that all who did not except their belief as the authorized religion of God was an infidel and did not deserve to live. We see this same religious and political mindset in the Bible in Acts 9:1-30 with the Apostle Paul who slew Christians in the name of Rome, but later became converted to live for a God who represented love.

Now getting to the subject of "hell," I will make references to the Bible because most people in our western world are familiar with stories of hell from the Bible—even though many other religions make references to hell. Most other religions speak of "hell" in some form or another, but they do not all believe "hell" to be a place of perpetual torment. Most religions do not use the word "hell" in reference to eternal retribution for wrong doings. Mainly those who are of the Christian based faith believe in hell as a literal place where evil-doers will burn forever for their non-repented sins, but this perspective is not shared with every other major religions.

There are five major religions practiced in the world today and they are: Islam, Hinduism, Judaism, Buddhism and Christianity. In reading other religious manuscript from the five major religions, Christianity and Islam are the only two of the five (that I remember) that teaches or believe in hell as a place of ever lasting punishment. The word "hell" in the Bible is a mistranslation of the Hebrew word "Sheol" which means the "pit" or better known as simply the "grave." Another mistranslation for the word hell found in the Bible is "Gehenna" known as the valley of the sons of Hinnom, where Israelites used to conduct abominable things like phallus worship (where they worshiped images of the male and female sexual organs) committed human sacrifice, rituals where children ran through burning coals barefoot and etc. Later "Gehenna" became known as a literal dumping ground or junkyard. When Jesus used the term "hell," He was referring to Gehenna (a dumping ground or junkyard) symbolically as the place where things go to simply never exist again. My personal belief is that this is a metaphoric place signifying the abolishment of evil consciousness. Jesus referenced this to the Israelites of the first century who would be thrown into the junk bin of history. I believe that Jesus was primarily in disgust with the Pharisees, Sadducees, Scribes just to name a few of the Jewish Sects and Orders of that time. These are the religious groups that Jesus continuously "bumped heads" with over doctrine. The Jewish Sects and Orders of that time had people confused about how to serve God—irritating Jesus to the hilt with their religious rules. This is why Jesus was considered a rebel among the religious world of His time, because He was not going to be placed into any of their religious categories. So Jesus referenced "hell" to the Israelites as a place where all the religious rhetoric, rituals, manipulations, and taking advantage of the poor would be laid to rest—or in other words, to be burned up and never seen again. This prediction however did come to pass around 67-70 AD when the Roman legions surrounded the city of Jerusalem and began to annihilate the Jewish stronghold. By the year 70 AD, the attackers had breached Jerusalem's outer walls and began a systematic neutralization of the city. The assault culminated in the burning and destruction of the Temple that served as the center of Judaism. I do not believe that Jesus was teaching a literal "hell" but was symbolically making reference to the demise of an abusive government that would be trampled beneath the earth—not to be remembered no more. I believe that "hell" being understood as the place for eternal suffering does not exists literally but exists metaphorically.

However, I do believe that hell's more literate meaning lies within the symbolism of a state of being—living in a state of perplexity, poverty, ignorance, sickness or any other situation defining the discomforts of life. On a personal level, hell can be a mindset of destitution—"For as a man believes in his heart so is he" (paraphrased) Proverbs 23:7—and Mathew 8:13 make a similar reference. However, religious leaders who intimidate others into converting to a particular faith did so by removing the symbolism of hell, and making it into a literal hell—a place of perpetual punishment for those who violate the commandments, or even the law of that day.

I believe that heaven—just like hell is also symbolic. When Jesus taught his disciples to pray in reference to heaven, it was with the anticipation that they would get the concept that heaven was within the human heart. Jesus taught his disciples to pray by saying; ". . . Thy kingdom come, thy will be done, on earth as it is in heaven." Matthew 6:10 KJV. If the *perceived will of God* is done on earth, there would be no need to "go to heaven,"—for peace and harmony among mankind would be present, making this heaven on earth. I believe that Jesus along with Buddha, Muhammad and the many other ancient patriots for peace on earth, taught the same message that heaven is within the human heart and not somewhere distant out in space. It does not matter the terminology they used for heaven because their message was a message of human wholeness.

We can, and will experience heaven and hell here on earth, but it is totally our choice which reality we choose to live in. We create our beds of reality by our perception of what is.

All of the major religions mentioned above agree that there is a God or Higher Intelligence, but none of them totally agree on the other basics like:

1. The number of Deities (how many Gods there are)
2. Gods gender
3. Reincarnation (life after death)
4. Nature of God (judgemental, benevolent, or neutral)
5. Path to salvation (good works, perfect karma, or Jesus)
6. Nature of the after life (heaven/hell, earth plane or to exist as energy.)

When we heighten our consciousness and become aware that we are the expression of Higher Intelligence in human form, we will indelibly become the controller of our earthly experiences. We will make our experience on earth heavenly and will bring unity to the world.

Article 43

Am I A Christian?

When I think of my friends and associates who profess Christianity, I am reminded of the diversities that lie within their individual beliefs. Each one of them sees the other as having habits, characteristics, or forms of worship/practices that disqualifies the other from being a Christian. This is because we have varied spiritual or religious backgrounds that have superimposed into our current belief systems. Every experience makes an impression upon our spirituality whether we are conscious of it or not. There is no way for us to separate our life experiences from our spirituality—they are one.

So am I a Christian? Well in most religious circles I would be considered a Christian, but I have come to a new reality of truth for myself that disconnects me from carrying any religious title. I consider myself as being one who live and walk in the awareness of God consciousness. If I allow myself to carry a title, then I subject myself to the proposed or expected behavior of others. I would be expected to live the way others believe that I should live—carrying the title of a Christian. I have chosen not to be defined by other people belief systems or religious practices—even though I have my own spiritual practices. I have discovered that I am a potpourri of many organized religious belief systems, but with each of them I disagree with one part or another which disqualifies me as being "true" to any of them. I take from each belief system what I believe is right for me and leave the rest for someone else who might prefer it. I personally see religions like a huge buffet where you place on your tray the food that you like, and whatever you do not prefer is someone else's preference.

Some would say that God has only one salvation plan that's tied up into one religious truth. I believe the Supreme Intelligence of the universe is too vast and too broad for one religion to embrace the wholeness of its deity. It is also my conviction that God, the Supreme Intelligence abides proportionately in each and every person, and is even disguised sometime as the most heinous individual—heinous at least from human perspective.

When I walk and live in the awareness that I am an intricate expression of God—not fearing others preconception of me—I am free to experience the fullness of the expression of the Supreme Intelligence abiding within me. I no longer aim to please the opinions of others or feel trapped in fulfilling the expectations of those who do not share my convictions. I am more profoundly governed by my awareness of living in the respect of my own convictions. I live reverently to the God who lives and speaks within the confines of my subconscious. My lifestyle is one that most people would consider respectful and honorable. I am proud of who I am—and striving to grow to my highest level of awareness. I Am Indeed Free!

What Is Prayer

As children many of us were given words to recite as a prayer—for instance: "Now I lay me down to sleep . . ." or "God is love, God is good, let us thank Him for our food . . . ," as stencils for prayers. Most of us are taught to pray to a God who is perceived to be out in space or far away in heaven. I believe that the God of the universe is presently abiding within our human vessels—our bodies. When we understand that God is never away from us—we will find ourselves empowered with the confidence that our prayers are always heard and answered.

Prayer has been given such complexity that many feel that praying is futile, and that only "holy people" are heard. Many believe that there is a certain way to pray or that they have to be bowed down on knees in order for the prayer to be genuine. None of this of course is true, but have rather given to the misconception that this is the prayer position. Much of this erroneous thinking has derived from the religious pictures of people kneeling with folded hands that we've seen from childhood. We have been inundated with the ideal that we must carry out certain rituals in order to be heard by God. Even pictures of a muscular God reaching down from heaven and touching the fingertip of a mere mortal man are all depictions of humans existing in a spiritually fallen state—in need of redemption. We have also seen the "Footstep in the Sand" pictures giving us the perception that God is some obscured entity invisibly lingering around, waiting to carry us when we get weak. It is a reassuring thought that there is someone who will help us when we are too weak to carry our burden. But the perception lends to this fallacy that God is outside of us.

We must become aware that there is no one particularly to bow down to, though many believe that this humble position shows reverence to Higher Intelligence. But I believe that true reverence is walking in the awareness or consciousness that God is in you and that you are in God and the two of you are one. There is no separation of human beings and Higher Intelligence—for humans alone with all of creation, are the expressions of God in material form. This is why Jesus repeated in St. John 14:19 saying (paraphrased) that "I am in the Father (God) and the Father is in me and we are one." Jesus also proclaims in prayer that his disciples become one with the Father (God) even as He is one with God. Becoming or being one with God is simply a matter of understanding that God speaks to us directly through and *from* our subconscious mind known as our spirit. It is to the subconscious mind or spirit or what I often refer to as the *inner self* (the place where God abides in human beings) that we pray, and not outside of ourselves.

God exists within us to communicate to us. When we beseech God, we are reaching for the voice of our own subconscious mind or *inner spirit*—which is the voice of God. This is why the Bible says that ". . . it is God who is at work within you, both to will (desire) and to do His good pleasure" (Philippians 2:13.) So your *inner self* (the place where God abides in you) already knows better than your conscious mind the things you need most. Therefore, it is unnecessary to continuously ask for the same thing over again—unless your repetition helps you achieve the level of belief where positive emotions flow. Sometimes repetition helps us to connect to our faith, but once belief and faith has been established, the only thing needed for manifestation is expectancy. When faith is actuated, the conscious mind can relax in knowing that the request is on the way.

So prayer should not be a ritual we do in order to get into God's good graces, but it is an encounter with our own God-potential. Prayer can also be understood as the expansion of our human creativity or the reestablishing of *self* to the infinite power of God found within our own being.

The final misconception about prayer is that prayer is a way of softening the heart of God and bringing ourselves to a level of worthiness. Nothing is further from the truth in my opinion. We are not here on earth to reach a place of heavenly rank, but to simply live out our creative abilities like the Higher Intelligence residing within us. Humans are gods having an earthly experience—attempting to manifest our God-potential through our everyday lives. We are collectively the expressions of the Universal Intelligence. There is no higher plain than that of awareness into our own divinity. So let us live our lives like the kings and queens we were created to be—walking with our heads high, knowing that our very existence is confirmation of the elect calling into worthiness and wonder.

God is as much of you—as salt is to the sea.

J. Meddling

45

Where Does Personal Convictions Come From?

Why do we have convictions or a consciousness of right and wrong? Where does this awareness come from? How does it relate or connect to our *sense of self*?

Almost every individual has an awareness of what's appropriate and inappropriate. Our concept of right and wrong stems from our childhood development. It later becomes our inner convictions after years of programming. Sometimes these inherent belief systems become challenged with new information as we evolve as spiritual beings—becoming enlightened to spiritual consciousness. When we evolve to that level of understanding our divinity, what we learned as a child as appropriate behavior sometimes conflicts with our *inner self*, the aspect of our *being* that connects us to the wisdom of God. This *inner self* is where I believe God abides within humans beings. Our *inner self* knows the truth of all things—even things we've never been taught in this life. The *inner self* can also be understood as being the subconscious, the spirit, or God within us.

It is within the confines of *self* that we relate to behaviors as acceptable and unacceptable. If we further dissect the root of this awareness, we will see that our personal *belief system* imparted to us as children forms our consciousness of right and wrong. What we believe dictates our actions which manifests into our behavior. But in the thinking process—before manifestation, our *belief system* again rules our perception of right and wrong. So in reality, our *belief system* is both responsible for our personal behavior as well as our perception of what's the appropriate behavior for others.

Personal convictions serve as a guiding force, protecting the moral essence of who we are. For example: Judy believes that cheating on taxes is wrong, but her friend Sherry says to her that "the government is always taking advantage of honest taxpayers, so you shouldn't feel bad claiming loss from your business that you really didn't incur—people do it all the time." But Judy declines the advice of her friend because Judy does not want to deal with feeling guilty about harboring a lie on her taxes. This is an example of a personal conviction protecting the moral essence of an individual. Refusing to do what one believes to be wrong to maintain a level of inner peace is the reality of living in the awareness of Godliness. If Judy had taken the advice of her friend Sherry, Judy would have violated her own personal convictions, leaving her to feel wounded in her perception of *self.* This is why many people seek the advice of others concerning their own personal matters. They have violated their own convictions so many times that they become scared with guilt—not feeling worthy to possess truth. This kind of guilt distances them from the inherited wisdom of God that abides in every human being. In the story of the Garden of Eden, it was guilt that caused Adam to distance himself from God—the same God who had always provided all things for Adam. Even if you do not believe the Garden of Eden story—the story of Adam hiding from God after eating from the forbidden tree—it still reflects the behaviors of people when they feel shame from a wrong done. An example of this is when you loan someone some money and they do not pay you back within the time agreed upon. Often the borrower has the tendency to avoid you—right? The shame or guilt of not having what is owed causes them to shun you. People who live guilt stricken lives often become dull to the voice of their personal convictions—thereby silencing the guiding voice of God. So when they pray to God, they cannot recognize the *voice* or language of God. The *voice* or language of God is heard and understood through our inner conscious. When we turn off the voice of our inner conscious (which is the voice of God)—we are turning away from the only true source of guidance. We turn off or disable this guiding source by violating our own convictions—doing the opposite of what we believe is right. To put it another way—not following your inner convictions is denouncing the God force abiding within you.

We should never behave outside of our moral belief system. Since there is such a diversity of beliefs and standards among human beings, one should live by their own convictions and not the conviction of another. Neither should we judge the conviction and belief systems of others, for there is multiformity in life experiences which mode every person's belief system.

As I stated earlier—how and what we believe as individuals is all based upon what we have experienced and what we've been taught. We cannot rightly judge the experiences that a person has in their life—and just as we reserve judgment of another person's experiences—so should we of their belief system.

Article 46

I Want To Be Free

(Don't Confine Me by Defining Me)

Many people take on titles and positions to wear as a status symbol or to give a sense of identity to who they are and what they believe. For example the title of being a Christian—in which this subject matter is relating to. If we live our lives in hope of simply obtaining what we perceive as impressive titles and loose focus on our life's purpose, we become confined and defined to a mere vanity. This is not to say that people take on the title of being a Christian just to have a status, but I do feel that they take on the title to give identification to a belief and a certain morality. Nevertheless, those who do confess any religion and are identified thereby subject themselves to the expectations of that belief system.

I believe that the *inner self* or God aspect of all human beings seeks to be free whether we live in this consciousness or not. When we take on a title or label, we become accountable to the observers and to those who may have appointed us with a position in a religious sect—i.e., relating to the appointment of a deacon, pastor, bishop or Arch bishop and etc. The responsibility of fulfilling the expectations that govern the lifestyle of one who holds these positions can often become a task. Fulfilling the expectation of others confines or enslave us to a behavior or lifestyle that we might find challenging to live out. Living the lives that we believe we are called to live should never feel like a task—because I personally believe that humans are innately free spirit *beings*. But when we fail to satisfy the expectation of the people who hold us to an obligation because of our title or position—we are often made to feel inadequate or unworthy. Their response to our perceived failure, emotionally subjects us to their power. We are therefore defined by someone else's expectation of appropriate actions and behaviors—which confines us to their belief system. I have discovered that people of the same religion still have various interpretations about what their religion is saying to them as individuals because of their various personal experiences with God—as I stated in article 43 **Am I A Christian?**.

When people say that they are Christians, they are viewed in a totally different light than someone who says that they are Agnostic or Atheist. This is because of the understanding of what these two belief systems consists of. A Christian's foundation is God/Christ, whereas the Agnostic and Atheist doubts or don't believe in the existence of God at all. We generally think of a Christian as being someone moral and benevolent—and one who does good deeds. I have observed that people who call themselves Christians fight against others who also profess Christianity—but who have different religious practices. We also hear of religious wars between groups of people who all believe that they are fighting for the cause of God, and yet they're fighting the same one's who also profess their love for God's righteousness. We witness a lot of religious chaos because people hold their own moral values or belief system above others beliefs. But none of them have a monopoly on what is *absolutely* right or wrong concerning their beliefs and values. If they indeed possessed the truth, concerning the matters they fight over, that would mean possessing the fullness of who God is—possessing a perfect understanding to the order of all things. My opinion is that it takes all of humanity working as one to fully embody the *person* of God. When we work as one people with a united mind we began to see and understand the truth, purpose and fullness of all things. We unfold the relevancy and *personhood* of God.

Once you define me—you confine me. We cannot progressively thrive as co-creators with God who is within us when we are confined to human expectations. God is the author of peace and harmony—attempting to live through all of us with individual expressions. Once we are given a title or label we become restricted to a perceived behavior that consequently revokes our ability to be free spirited. Jesus himself had to refuse the expectations of those who thought that He should become their king after he had fed five thousand with five loaves of bred and two small fish. But the time had not come for Jesus to be recognized as a king (referred to in St. John 6:1-15).

There is absolutely nothing wrong with being *defined* and *confined* as long as we understand the responsibility that comes with that label. We must also be willing to be under the scrutiny of onlookers. We should however know whether or not this is our season to handle the potential aggressions of people with contrasting opinions or views—just as Jesus knew His season to be acknowledged as king. Every leader should be mindful of the influence they have on others. Though every mature and independent thinker should take responsibility for themselves, many do not. We who are strong must indeed help bear the infirmity of the weak. Unfortunately many people in authority forget this basic premise of leadership. I believe this is the reason for so many of our religious and political leaders being ridiculed—being caught doing things that do not reflect the perceived moral standards of the title they carry. We are all believed to be guilty of having faults and wrong doings—so having labels and titles will not eradicate our imperfections. Since this is the case, why do we harshly judge people based upon our own moral expectations when we understand that we are *perceivably* innately flawed by our humanity? It is because the title carries the weight of responsibility. I believe that many of these expectations are unrealistic for anyone to perfectly achieve. However, I am not advocating living without moral restraints, because I strongly believe that leaders and people in "power" should be held to a higher standard because they have chosen to be in the spotlight of ridicule and scrutiny. However, I do believe that we should always stay focus on being true to our own convictions—and not allowing ourselves to be devastated or even worried by the actions of others. We should always be true to ourselves, and be responsible for our own lives—not dictated by the actions of others. I have heard many great athletes state that they are not trying to be anyone's "role model." Their consensus is the idea of not trying to live up to others expectations. The thought of trying not to fail anyone's expectations is more responsibility than anyone should have to bear. It is not likely that any of us can suit the need and expectations of others and maintain our own sense of freedom.

I have recently heard of more people in relationships saying that they want to be free from the traditional expectations and titles that typically define relationships. They are not seeking to be free from the relationship—but not wanting to have a title such as husband or wife, boyfriend or girlfriend connected to them. People are redefining relationships all over the world. One example of this are married couples who live in separate houses and who are very content with this arrangement (usually couples in their 40s and up). And what about "open marriages" where a couple agrees to have other sexual partners by one another's consent? So we can see how the dynamics of traditional titles and expectations have changed even in relationships. Though I am not endorsing any of these arrangements, I can not help but realize that people are attempting to maintain their personal identity by not allowing themselves to be confined to cultural norms or the norms of relationships or by the expectations of others. Relationships have a totally new dynamic than in the earlier years of the Baby Boomers—and it's working for a lot of couples. If we choose not to be confined to other's expectations, then let's not harness ourselves to titles and labels. We should live our lives to our own expectations and enjoy being a free spirit.

Article 47

Understanding *Self* in the Family Unit
(Tribute to my family)

I am reminded of my childhood days as a seven year old boy who was awaken on a school morning by the aroma of bacon and eggs, pancakes and oatmeal being prepared. It was always the smell of breakfast cooking that would wake me and my six siblings—signifying that it was time to get up and prepare for school. My mother would awaken before sunrise to prepare a breakfast fit for a king's table, for her husband and seven children. Not only did she arise early to prepare breakfast, but made sure that we got our dose of cod liver oil—that was chased with a glass of orange juice. Mother would line me and my siblings up like little soldiers to give us our daily dose of the cheapest cold and flu preventive known during the sixties. She would see us off to school one-by-one with a kiss on each of our cheeks. Not only would she see us off, but would be waiting on the porch or at the front door when we came home from school. I did not think about it as a child, but thinking back on those moments as an adult, it was always an assuring feeling coming home and seeing mother smiling on the porch. It was as if she had been waiting all day for our return from school. There was always a treat to come home to. Again, the meal would already be on the kitchen table—steaming hot. Mother always validated me and my siblings with the love that she showed in her every-day routine of caring for us.

As a young boy growing up with a severe speech impediment and learning disorder, my mother would encourage me by saying *"one day you will rule the world."* What she really meant was that one day I would not be dictated by my inadequacies, and that I would rise above the disappointments of being a slow learner. As a child, those words continuously rang in my soul. Today, I am no longer haunted by the fears of inadequateness of speech or stuttering—for the reality of my *higher self* or the God in me came alive through my mother's encouragement. As an adult, I still hear the voice of God through my mother's words. My sense of *self* and awareness of God is a direct manifestation of my mother's encouragement. Little did I know then, that in this small house full of so much love and encouragement would come the beginning of me learning *wholeness*.

The small three bed room and one bath house, that gave shelter to seven children and two parents, always embodied the fresh scent of pine-sol and lemon furniture polish. Though we were poor by society standards, we felt like the richest kids on earth. As a matter of fact, we as children did not know that we were classified as poor because we had both mother and father in the home that showed their affection to us as well as to one another. I fondly remember my mother and father playfully wrestling with each other on the living room floor, and my siblings and I watching and laughing hysterically. We were wondering who would win the wrestling match between mom and dad, because mom was a farm girl raised with three brothers and knew how to rough-house with the best of them. My father on the other hand was a small man—much smaller than my mother. Often mother won the wrestling match—I guess daddy let her win. I also remember the family outings at the lake where mother had already prepared lunches for all the children and daddy had the duty of getting the fishing poles ready to catch the fish that we would later have for dinner. We would spend the whole day outside entertained by the simple unity of our family. In those days, it did not take much for children to have fun.

I remember how my father would take the family out for entertainment which was no more than a car ride around the town usually. I was about five or six and daddy would take the family riding because we didn't have the money to go to an amusement park—so our recreation was just riding around in the car. I would stand on the back seat and make animated sounds when he turned the car sharply around corners—scrrrrrrrrrr was the sound I made around every sharp turn. This was before children had to be buckled with seatbelts. I never told my daddy, but that was one of my favorite recreations.

How about that time—I was around seven and he took the family fishing and I was afraid to bate my hook? I did not know that he was aware of my fear of bating the worm onto the hook, but he gently took my fishing poll and with a confident smile hooked the worm so that I could fish with the older siblings. I did not tell my father, but that day he was my hero.

I remember when daddy told me to stop throwing rocks at the birds early one Sunday morning. I was only eight standing beside the family car waiting for the rest of the family to come out and load up for church. But when my father went into the house to gather the rest of the family for church, I threw that last rock anyway and wounded a baby bird. I had hoped that daddy wouldn't see the little bird in the bushes flopping and screeching in agony. But he did, and asked me "Why did you hit that innocent baby bird?" All I could answer was, "I don't know." Instead of whipping me like I thought he would, daddy made me watch that baby bird suffer as my punishment. The poor wounded baby bird unable to fly or stand, screeching hysterically until it came to a diminishing weak chirp and finally died. I never told my dad, but that was the worst punishment that I could have ever gotten. And I never told him how that on that day—it made me appreciative of all life—even little birdies.

At the age of twelve when I joined my first church, and as I nervously walked down the church isle—I remember the proud look that my dad gave me. I did not tell him, but the look on his face gave me validation as a young man. On that day I felt confident in making my own decisions.

Around age fourteen I came to my father confused about the interpretation of a Bible verse. Though dad was busy doing upholstery, in which he was always preoccupied with to make extra money to support our family, being the great provider he's always been—daddy put his hammer down, sat on a stool facing me and took the time to explain in detail the meaning of that scripture. My father has always been an excellent teacher. I did not tell him, but I knew on that day that I too wanted to be a teacher of the Bible just like him.

Daddy was a fix-it-man too. I remember when the water heater went out and he decided to replace it himself—knowing that it was a potentially dangerous job for a first-timer. But he took the challenge and replaced it himself. We all left the house except for mother when he turned on the power to the unit. We trusted that he knew what he was doing—but just in case.

And how about the time the roof was leaking and to save money that we did not have to spend, daddy took on a roof repair single handedly. Yeah, he fell through the roof with his legs dangling through the kitchen ceiling hanging over mothers pot of soup that she had cooking on the stove. But daddy fixed that roof by himself! I never told him, but seeing how he would take on projects and complete them assured me that I would one day be that same "fix-it man" too.

When I was only sixteen, I remember coming to my father embarrassed and disappointed with myself. I told my dad that I had gotten a young woman pregnant, and I would soon be a father. I saw the disappointment on his face but heard the firm encouragement in daddy's voice when he said to me "Men in this family take care of their responsibilities." Though I was young, I perfectly understood that I had placed myself into a man's position, and that I could no longer live the life of a boy. The real life experience of raising a child was now my new reality. I did not tell him, but I knew that day, because of his encouraging words that I would be the best father I could be.

It has been through the support of my family unit, the portrayed strength of my father, and the nurturing love of my mother who has now transitioned from this life—that has made me the man I am today. I learned to show compassion to all people, through the compassion I saw my parents show to others. I have seen my parents bring in strangers from off the street and sit them down at our dinner table.

I fondly remember how mother not only made special treats for me and my siblings, but for the neighborhood kids as well. She was affectionately called "the pie lady" by the children in our community. I learned to have an appreciation for all God's people and even God's creatures through the lesson my father taught me when I killed the baby bird with the rock. When I reflect back to that experience of killing that bird—it shows me how so many people suffer affliction as a result of another's pleasure, sport, or vindictiveness. I learned to value all life, and to bear other's opinions and lifestyles—no matter how different it is from my own. I learned from my mother how to nurture the human soul, and how that all life blossoms when watered with love. I learned from her that no person is a waste of time. With my learning disability and speech impediment as a child, my mother validated me and assured me with her smile and touch that I could accomplish anything. She always looked at me so proudly—and through her eyes I found confidence.

The simplistic love of the family unit is almost a lost art in our western culture—of busy lives and high-tech toys. Maintaining the family as a unit is an "art" because it takes the creativity of loving parents to nurture the intricate balance of wholeness in a child. Our inner constitution or the convictions that we own—is first established by the influences of our parents in the early childhood years. It is later that our unconscious influences (the things we were taught as a child, but may not consciously remember now), manifest into the behavior that we display as adults. Our understanding of our *inner self*—the place where God dwells, is primarily formed by the perception of those who influenced us as children. Simply speaking—we see or understand God through the eyes of our parents, mentors or influencers. We believe that we are who we are by the words we are told from those we respect. Our *sense of self* is delicately balanced on the impression that we are able to project to others as well as their impression projected onto us. We are creatures of community who thrive on feeling accepted by those we admire, respect and simply love. This is why the family unit is so crucial to the *self* being whole. Parents who nurture their children are teaching them to be nurtures to the world around them.

There is no greater influence in our lives than the influence of the family unit—no matter the dynamics of the family. This is the foundation of all future potentials. The influence of the family is where birth is given to our belief systems. Our belief system is what anchors us to our inner convictions. Therefore, let us appreciate the expressed love of God manifested in the family unit.

A nation is as strong as the families it embodies.
J. Meddling